A Teacher's Guide to

Working with Paraeducators and Other Classroom Aides

Jill Morgan
and
Betty Y. Ashbaker

**ASSOCIATION FOR SUPERVISION
AND CURRICULUM DEVELOPMENT**

Alexandria, Virginia USA

Association for Supervision and Curriculum Development
1703 N. Beauregard St. • Alexandria, VA 22311-1714 USA
Telephone: 1-800-933-2723 or 703-578-9600 • Fax: 703-575-5400
Web site: http://www.ascd.org • E-mail: member@ascd.org

Printed in the United States of America.

February 2001 member book (p). ASCD Premium, Comprehensive, and Regular members periodically receive ASCD books as part of their membership benefits. No. FY01-05.

ASCD Product No. 100236
ASCD member price: $15.95   nonmember price: $18.95

Library of Congress Cataloging-in-Publication Data
Morgan, Jill, 1956-
  A teacher's guide to working with paraeducators and other classroom aides / Jill Morgan and Betty Y. Ashbaker.
      p. cm.
"ASCD product no. 100236"—T.p. verso.
Includes bibliographical references and index.
  ISBN 0-87120-505-X (alk. paper)
  1. Teachers' assistants—Training of—United States—Handbooks, manuals, etc. 2. Teaching teams—United States—Handbooks, manuals, etc. I. Ashbaker, Betty Y., 1950- II. Title.
  LB2844.1.A8 M66 2001
  371.14'124—dc21
                        00-011679

07 06 05 04 03 02 01   10 9 8 7 6 5 4 3 2 1

A Teacher's Guide to Working with Paraeducators and Other Classroom Aides

Introduction

This book addresses what is considered a "new" role for teachers: supervising paraeducators. If you feel that this is a role for which you were not prepared in your undergraduate teacher training, you are not alone. Most teachers have received no such preparation, although they (and you) may have often worked with paraeducators at practicum sites or during student teaching placements. Even special education teachers—who regularly work with paraeducators— typically receive little training in working with other adults.

There are good reasons for a book addressing this so-called new role for teachers. First, the number of paraeducators working in schools across the United States has increased substantially in the last 15 years. Second, although we agree with the belief of many people that adults should, and generally do, work things out between themselves, we also believe that working together as adults involves many skills, and even the most willing and experienced teachers and paraeducators can learn to work together more effectively. This book will cover the basic skills that you as a teacher need to make the best use of the wonderful human resource that paraeducators represent for our schools and our children.

We use the term *paraeducator* as the most up-to-date term being applied to the people you may call aides, teaching assistants, instructional assistants, or by a variety of other titles. The term *paraeducator* was coined by Anna Lou Pickett (1997), director of the National Resource Center for Paraprofessionals in New

Portions of this chapter were published previously in Ashbaker, B., & Morgan, J. (1997, April). Teachers, what's your supervision style? *Theories and Practices in Supervision and Curriculum (Journal of the Utah ASCD)* viii: 34–37. Reprinted by permission of the editor.

York, and it mirrors titles such as *paralegal* and *paramedic* to designate someone who works alongside *(para)* a professional in the legal, medical, or (in this case) education field.

The principles of effective supervision we describe in this book apply equally to any adults who may work in your classroom—parent or grandparent volunteers, student teachers, and others. We refer to your paraeducator as "she" because more than 90 percent of paraeducators employed across the United States are female. We also refer to "your paraeducator" in the singular, although you may in fact work with more than one paraeducator or other adult. The principles of effective supervision are the same, although your managerial responsibilities are obviously more extensive and could take more time and effort.

The paraeducator assigned to you may be older or younger than you; she may have a high school diploma or full teaching qualifications. She may come with many years of experience as a parent, 4-H leader, businessperson, or den leader; or she may be fresh out of high school. Her role may be largely clerical, but more typically these days she plays an integral role in the instructional process. The important distinction is that you as the teacher have overall responsibility for the classroom and the students assigned to you, and your paraeducator works under your direction. As the classroom "executive," you have overall responsibility whether the paraeducator works in your classroom under your direct supervision, works with students from your class but in another area of the school building, or comes to your classroom for only part of the day accompanying a special education student. The same principles of good supervision apply to all of these situations.

An Overview of the Book

As the teacher, only you can make certain decisions—executive decisions that reflect your qualifications and professional responsibilities. However, you can, and should, share the task of carrying out those decisions with other adults who work in the classroom once they have received proper training and clear expectations have been set. The responsibility for ensuring that students receive appropriate instruction, for example, belongs to you, but the daily task of delivering that instruction can be a shared responsibility.

Chapter 1 looks at your responsibilities as the leader of the classroom instructional team and the ways in which your "new" role as a supervisor of other adults can mesh with the more traditional teacher role of supervisor of curriculum and instruction. Recently, considerable talk has focused on the notion of equality among educators, particularly in relation to teachers and paraeducators. Each member of the team is equally important in the sense that the success of the joint effort depends upon both individuals taking their responsibilities seriously and making a best effort in their respective roles. But in reality, teachers and paraeducators are not equal in many ways. Legally they are not equal in the degree of responsibility or accountability assigned to them, nor are they considered equal professionally with regard to the education of children. Each member of the education team needs to have clearly defined roles—some individual and some shared. Fortunately, members of a team do not have to be equal in all aspects to function efficiently and deliver appropriate educational services.

Chapter 2 takes you through the process of identifying the roles and responsibilities you will assign to your paraeducator and explains how to clarify them so that your paraeducator has a clear idea of what your expectations are and of what she can expect from you. If you supervise more than one paraeducator, you will need to define the roles and responsibilities of each member of the team. Developing and communicating roles and responsibilities to more than one paraeducator will require much more time initially, but the effort will prevent potential "turf" problems and unnecessary duplication of resources later. In later chapters on monitoring your paraeducator and providing feedback and training, we discuss ways in which you can have your paraeducators work together if you are fortunate enough to be assigned more than one.

Chapter 3 considers the different approaches and experiences adults bring to the classroom and how those factors influence effective communication. Our definition of *communication* is comprehensive and includes a person's whole approach to what they do, not merely what they say and how they say it.

Chapters 4, 5, and 6 take you through the processes of assessing your paraeducator's skills and abilities, providing on-the-job training, and establishing a procedure for giving and receiving feedback from your paraeducator on her work. The processes described in these chapters parallel the effective instructional practices that you use every day with your students as you first assess and then build on their skills and knowledge. You also make them an active participant in the process, helping them to become more aware of the learning taking place and supporting them as they take increasing responsibility for their own learning. These practices are directly applicable to your work with another adult.

The remaining chapters deal with practical concerns, such as the integration of these procedures into your already busy schedule and how to deal with the supervisory difficulties that may arise despite your best efforts. At the end of the book we include a brief list of resources related to training and support for paraeducators.

At the end of Chapters 1 through 7 is a section entitled "In Practice," which offers suggestions on how you can translate the subject matter of the chapter into your own classroom situation, as well as a fill-in-the-blank form that can serve as the basis of a self-improvement plan and help you to set personal goals related to your supervisory role. This book is intended to be a practical guide and workbook. The chapters offer many opportunities to reflect on what you do and analyze what you have read. Make the most of these opportunities; they will assist your learning, facilitate your goal setting, and ultimately help you enhance your skills as a supervisor of classroom practice and instruction.

The ideas in this book come from many years of direct experience in working with teachers and paraeducators as they increase their effectiveness as instructional teams. Some of the ideas also come from other disciplines, such as business and management. Most important, they have been tried and approved by classroom practitioners. It is important to share many of the ideas in this book with your paraeducator, because both of you will need to develop certain skills and work together on becoming a more effective team. Having another adult in the classroom can be a rewarding and valuable experience. It offers exciting prospects for enhancing student learning as well as your own practices as a teacher.

Determining Your Personal Supervisory Style

Whether the supervisory role is new to you or you have been a supervisor of paraeducators or other adults for some time, you probably have a fairly definite idea of how people "should" be supervised. Try the following exercise. Read the situation outlined below and the three supervision approaches—A, B, and C—that follow. Then respond to the questions.

Supervising Mrs. P.

You have just begun a job as an elementary school teacher in a rural district. At the end of your first week with the class, you look back and mentally evaluate how things went and what might need to be changed. On the whole, you are pleased with your new class. They are the usual mix of 4th graders with lively minds and bodies, and you accomplished most of what you had planned. It seems that you can look forward to an enjoyable and challenging year. You have been assigned a student with learning disabilities, who spends about half of the day in your classroom with his assigned paraeducator and half in the resource room, but the other children seem to know and accept him, and you think the situation will work out OK.

But that reminds you of something that has been bothering you more and more as the week has progressed: Mrs. P., the paraeducator assigned to the student with learning disabilities. She is a very pleasant woman, some years older than you, who let you know almost immediately when she introduced herself how much experience she had, how well she knew the school and the pupils, and that she was the superintendent's wife. Somehow her reassurance that you didn't need to worry about her at all—she and her assigned pupil would be no trouble and you could act as if they weren't even there—raised more concerns than it resolved. She was indeed very helpful and capable that first day, but you had the strong feeling that you were not to encroach on her territory and that she didn't want or need any direction from you to get her job done. And as the days passed, that impression deepened. She arrived promptly every morning and capably but firmly managed her charge, taking initiative but cheerfully refusing assistance and making small decisions without consulting you. She made it clear that her presence in the classroom was not to be viewed as an extra pair of hands, but that her responsibilities were limited to her pupil and ended abruptly at the end of the integration session.

As you look back over the first week and adjust your plans for the rest of the semester, what approach will you take to the supervision of this paraeducator? Will you take the approach of Supervisor A, B, or C?

Supervisor A

You realize that Mrs. P. not only is considerably older than you but also has had more classroom experience and obviously knows the students and the community much better than you do, as a newcomer. She seems to be very capable, keeps her assigned student busy on the tasks that you set, has a pleasant and positive style, and bears the brunt of the responsibility for a student who might otherwise prove to be a little difficult. You don't want to upset her, because she is so helpful. And anyway, you may just be overreacting to her independence, because you've never had a paraeducator assigned to your classroom in this way before. The idea of even having to supervise someone who is so capable seems a little ridiculous.

You decide to check with her regularly to see that she understands what you would like her to do. There never seems to be time to discuss the day's planned activities when she arrives, and you know that when she leaves the classroom, the student returns to the resource room and her working day ends, and so you can't ask her to stay behind and talk to you. But she hasn't had any trouble picking up on assignments, and so you decide to write out a sheet of planned activities each week, to give to her first thing Monday morning. In this way she at least will know what will be happening a few days ahead. In fact, you could probably get it to her on Friday so that she has some advance notice and can ask you any questions she has about it on Monday. If you also talk regularly to the resource room teacher about what you are doing and coordinate things with her, you'll have a good idea of how things are working out for the student.

Supervisor B

Although Mrs. P. is very capable and cheerfully assists her student and keeps him busy all day, the fact that she seems to regard him as "her" student doesn't sit well with your philosophy that you are responsible for all of the students in your classroom. You feel as if you're not really the one in charge or in control. You see the student's work when it's finished, but you haven't yet been able to watch him as he works, and so you don't know how he handles the assignments and how much he relies on—or is helped by—Mrs. P. She seems to protect him, and you would like to see him develop some independence and confidence in his own ability to succeed without so much help.

You decide to tell her that you want to work with him sometimes and that she can perhaps do some preparation work; if she doesn't consider it to be part of her job to help the other students in the class or help you with your preparation, she can still do things that need to be done for her assigned student. If you give her a sheet that lists the times when you want to work with the student and also tell her that you want him sometimes to join the rest of the class without her help, she can plan to do preparation during those times. You can give her the sheet on Monday morning when she comes in.

Supervisor C

You view the students and the adults in the classroom as your responsibility, but also as resources and coparticipants in the education process. As you see it, you need to make best use of everyone's talents and abilities so that the maximum possible learning takes place. With her knowledge of the school and the community, Mrs. P. is obviously going to be a real asset in helping you to meet the needs of the students. Her dedication and commitment are admirable, and you anticipate a year in which a lot can be accomplished. Mrs. P.'s schedule doesn't include any time for planning with you as a team, and you'll have to talk to the administrator about that. Meanwhile, it shouldn't be too difficult to set a mutually convenient time once a week when the two of you can sit together and do some planning while the student works independently. Mrs. P.'s input will be very valuable.

Advantages and Disadvantages of A, B, and C

Which approach would you take—A, B, or C? _____

What do you see as the advantages and disadvantages of the three approaches?

Approach A
Advantages

_____

_____

_____

_____

Disadvantages

_____

_____

_____

_____

Approach B
Advantages

_____

_____

_____

_____

Disadvantages

_____

_____

_____

_____

Approach C
Advantages

_____

_____

_____

_____

Disadvantages

_____

_____

_____

_____

Whichever approach you take—or even if you take an entirely different approach—you, the classroom teacher, are ultimately responsible for what takes place in the classroom. You can select a supervision style that suits you, just as you select curriculum and teaching techniques that suit your own preferences as well as your students' needs. Your teacher education training and student teaching focused on the need to use your knowledge of validated curriculum and instructional practices to ensure student achievement. This responsibility cannot be abdicated to an untrained or uncertified staff member.

By completing the preceding exercise and identifying the supervision style that you think would work best for you, your students, and the paraeducator described, you are taking the first step in preventing some of the complications of working with another adult in the classroom before they occur. Identifying your style should also help you to begin the process of defining and clarifying your supervisory role; the following chapters and their activities can assist you.

Leading the Classroom Instructional Team

1

Before you can effectively supervise your paraeducator, it is important that you understand your responsibilities as leader of the classroom instructional team and how those responsibilities mesh together for the benefit of students. This chapter will help you to do so. It will also help you explore your current approach to the supervision of adults and consider how you and the students can fully benefit from having a paraeducator working with you in the classroom. In this chapter we address these questions:

- What are your responsibilities as the leader of an instructional team?
- How can you make the best use of your paraeducator and the valuable skills and experience she brings to the classroom?
- How do you relate instructional goals for your students to your responsibilities as the supervisor of a paraeducator?
- How does validated curriculum relate to your dual role and responsibilities for instruction of students and supervision of paraeducators?

Understanding Your Leadership Responsibilities

What are your responsibilities as the leader of an instructional team? David Berliner (1989) has suggested that today's teacher has essentially become an executive, with duties closely resembling those of executives in business and management. He sees this as being a result of the increasing numbers of paraeducators and volunteers who work in today's classrooms, and he lists nine "executive functions" of a teacher's role:

- Planning work
- Communicating goals
- Regulating the activities of the workplace
- Creating a pleasant environment for work
- Educating new members of the work group
- Articulating with other units in the system
- Supervising and working with other people
- Motivating those being supervised
- Evaluating the performance of those being supervised

As the leader of an instructional team, you are responsible for these areas in relation both to students and to your paraeducator.

When teachers are the only adults in the classroom working directly with students, they are the only adult authority figures and are solely responsible for ensuring an environment that is conducive to learning. They direct all of the learning activities and establish and maintain an effective classroom management structure. The introduction of another adult into the classroom adds a management level and complicates the functioning of the classroom—although it also brings major benefits for you and your students when handled properly. If you delegate some of the responsibility for instruction to your paraeducator, you must be sure that she is competent. Because you both have contact with students, you share classroom management roles. And because students also have another adult to refer to, you must ensure that the paraeducator adheres to the same behavior management and instructional procedures that you use, and that students do not receive conflicting messages about work and behavior. Regulating classroom activities requires that you carefully plan your goals and use effective communication with both adults and students.

These executive functions can be time-consuming, and you probably have no desire to become an executive instead of a teacher. (Most teachers say that they chose the profession because they want to teach students.) Completing the activities in this book will help you to combine the roles and incorporate executive skills into your repertoire of teaching skills so that you can focus on student learn-ing and face fewer distractions related to management tasks. Many of the skills you will acquire have been well defined and are highly valued in other fields, such as business; like education, these fields require collaboration on providing services to others, supervision, and so on. The skills are based on well-validated principles that you will apply to the classroom—the place where services are delivered directly to students. It is crucial that the best possible practices be used in the classroom, and that you, as the teacher and supervisor of both students and other adults, master the practices and skills that will help to ensure student success. As you complete the activities in this book, you will learn new skills, but you should also begin to recognize that many things you already do are supervisory practices, and many of the skills you use with students are directly applicable to your work with paraeducators.

Richard Learn (1988) has pointed out that the term *supervision* has many dif-ferent definitions. Take a moment to think about and then write your personal definition of the term *supervision* in relation to other adults in your classroom.

In relation to other adults, I see supervision as

_____

_____

_____

_____

_____

_____

_____

_____

Some authors define supervision as control and management to ensure effective and economical use of human resources (such as paraeducators). Others define it as orientation and inservice training. And yet others see it as helping employees to improve their own performance in their assigned duties. The particular situation in which you work as a teacher may emphasize one of these views more than another, but all of these definitions are valid: the teacher is responsible for effective and wise use of a valuable human resource. This includes orienting paraeducators to their assigned roles, with ongoing training, so that you can make the best possible use of their time and skills to help your instructional team meet the goal of student success.

Making the Best Use of Your Paraeducator

How can you make the best use of your paraeducator and the valuable skills and experience she brings to the classroom? Sergiovanni and Starratt (1993) have suggested that we need to revise our whole approach to supervision by involving all of those concerned and building a common vision of what we wish to achieve together. Although Sergiovanni and Starratt most often focus on the whole school as the learning community, the same principles can be applied to the classroom, where all of those concerned can be involved in decision making and in working toward a common vision, and where human resources are developed to the fullest extent. This goes far deeper than the level of human relationships, where concerns include cooperative attitudes and nondiscriminatory practices. Berliner (1989) covers these when he talks about creating pleasant and motivating environments for work. Here we are concerned with the development of human resources: supervisory practices that help to develop the skills and knowledge of each person who works in the classroom and forms part of the instructional team. Hofmeister (1991) has suggested that we are doing our paraeducators and our students a significant disservice if we do not provide proper supervision, support, and training to enable the paraeducators to acquire the skills they need to work effectively. In later chapters we focus on the teacher's role of monitoring the quality of work and providing on-the-job training to help paraeducators develop their own skills. These are all part of the responsibilities of the teacher as an executive and supervisor of adults.

Your paraeducator is a valuable human resource, not only because she represents an extra pair of hands and eyes in the classroom, but because of the experience and skills that she brings to her role as part of the instructional team. This might be a good moment to think about your paraeducator. Write down what you know about her and how you feel her experience can contribute to the classroom. Remember, if she is in her 30s or 40s, she may bring a great deal of life experience, but even a younger paraeducator can make substantial contributions: her very inexperience may enable her to see things quite differently from you and offer a fresh perspective. Consider cultural and travel experiences, child rearing, and other employment experience that your paraeducator may have. If you find it difficult to write much here because you know very little about your paraeducator, that realization should prompt you to find out more. As you learn about her strengths and areas of exceptional talent or experience, you can offer her instructional opportunities that allow her to share her skills and experience with students.

What I know about my paraeducator:

_____

_____

_____

_____

_____

_____

How this might contribute to her work:

_____

_____

_____

_____

_____

_____

You can also ask your paraeducator if there are other areas in which she would like to share her skills or ideas. Add those to the list.

Relating Instructional Goals to Supervisory Responsibilities

How do you relate instructional goals for your students to your responsibilities as the supervisor of a paraeducator? One of the executive functions of the teacher's role listed by David Berliner was "communicating goals." We talk about communication in Chapter 3, but take a moment now to think about your instructional goals and how they relate to your work with your paraeducator. What are your instructional goals for this school year or semester? List some of them below.

1. _____
2. _____
3. _____
4. _____
5. _____

You may have some very broad instructional and curricular goals for the school year: teaching students about the U.S. Civil War, for example, or providing a safe environment in which students feel secure enough to learn and grow. And those goals can, of course, be broken down into more specific objectives: helping students understand the causes of the Civil War, or establishing clear expectations for behavior in the classroom. When you work with a paraeducator or another adult in the classroom, these goals become the paraeducator's as well; as she assists you in providing instruction and managing the learning environment, she needs to know what those goals are and what her role is in helping you accomplish those goals. As you read Chapter 2 (Assigning Roles and Responsibilities) and complete the activities included in it, bear in mind that the whole purpose of having the assistance of a paraeducator is to help you accomplish your goals for the students. If she has a clear picture of what you are trying to accomplish, the roles that you assign her will make more sense to her. They will have a context, and she will be able to see them as part of a larger plan.

How Validated Curriculum Fits In

How does validated curriculum relate to your dual role and responsibilities for instruction of students and supervision of paraeducators? We have already stated that although many of your classroom responsibilities can—and should—be shared with your paraeducator, some responsibilities are primarily or solely yours. The selection and modification of curriculum is a responsibility that is yours (perhaps in tandem with the school instructional leader). The curriculum directly affects your work as a supervisor of other adults in the classroom, therefore we will take time to review some basic principles before relating them to supervision. We make two premises:

1. Teaching is as much a science as an art. Although some people may have more of a natural flair for it than others, it can be learned and effectively practiced by all who are involved in the education process.
2. All that we do as educators is ultimately for the benefit of the students. Whatever improvements or changes we seek to make, our ultimate aim is to increase the likelihood of student success and to provide an environment conducive to learning.

The executive functions of teaching as expressed by David Berliner are important to all teachers, whether or not they supervise other adults in their classroom. However, supervising others highlights the need to be able to carry out these functions as part of your daily routine as well as communicate their importance to your paraeducator. For example, it is possible to work through a curriculum without a clear idea of exactly where you are heading or how you are going to get there (although we would not recommend doing it!). However, when you share your work with another adult and you have to explain the objectives and goals of that curriculum, it becomes far more important to have a clear idea of what is intended and to be able to express that idea. You cannot communicate objectives that you have not formulated or make a valid assessment of progress toward goals that you have not identified. This is true of your work with students and with other adults in the classroom. Supervisory responsibilities highlight the need for the basic skills of an effective educator.

We refer here to the notion of validated curriculum as a reminder that your first responsibility is to provide instruction to students, using curriculum that (1) is appropriate to the students' needs, and (2) has been properly validated— that is, subjected to rigorous testing before marketing and use. Curriculum validation is a lengthy and expensive process and is not generally considered to be your responsibility as a teacher. However, recognizing effective and less effective curriculum and methodology is within your area of expertise. You can see which programs and methods work best with your students. As a teacher who supervises one or more paraeducators, you must not only make adjustments to the prescribed curriculum to meet a particular student's needs and enhance learning, but also teach your paraeducator to recognize such effective practice and use it as she works with students.

This adds yet another dimension to supervision: as the professional educator you are a role model for your paraeducator. You are an example of how to deliver instruction effectively and how to manage the classroom so that it provides an environment conducive to student learning. You also provide a role model of professionalism as you show your willingness to constantly examine your own effectiveness and improve your practice. This is one of the most important things you can do for your paraeducator. As you share your enthusiasm for your work and involve her in problem solving to provide the best possible education for the students, you will also provide her with opportunities to grow in an environment conducive to adult learning.

Summary

This chapter, indeed the whole book, is intended to improve your executive practices as an educator who supervises paraeducators for the ultimate benefit of your students. We work on the assumption that student achievement is your primary purpose and that you believe that you can—and should—constantly seek to enhance your skills as an educator. As a supervisor of another adult in the classroom, you may be able to adapt some of the skills that you already possess, and you may need to acquire others; but you will be a role model for your paraeducator and enable her to acquire new skills also, so that your work together as an instructional team is enhanced to the greatest possible extent.

In Practice

Following are some suggestions for ways in which you can apply what you have learned in this chapter to your own working situation. We also have provided space for you to add ideas that you glean from your own experience and interactions with colleagues.

• As a sign of recognition that your paraeducator is an integral member of the classroom team, post her name outside the classroom door along with yours. It sends a message to students and adults in the school that you value her, that her efforts and authority are to be recognized and respected, and that it is her classroom as well as yours.

• Take time to talk to your paraeducator about how she views your work together. Does she see herself as being an important part of the team? What does she see as the advantages of working as part of a team? What does she think are the characteristics of a successful and effective team? You might also wish to consider your answers to these questions before you seek her opinions. Consider designing a shield or choosing a motto for your team. You can cut a piece of poster paper in the shape of a shield, divide it into three or four sections, and draw something in each of those sections to denote one of your team goals or something else that represents your values as an instructional team—a photograph of the class, for example, or something to represent diversity. When you work on this sort of activity together, especially if you work with more than one paraeducator, it helps to give the whole group a sense of identity and common purpose.

- _____

_____

_____

- _____

_____

_____

- _____

_____

_____

Setting Priorities for Improvement

Now that you have read about leading the instructional team and have had an opportunity to consider how this applies to the situation you work in, take some time to set priorities for your work in this area. Choose one aspect of leading the instructional team, list one or two ways in which you think you can improve in this area, decide how you will know if you have made improvements, determine ways in which you might keep a record and use it to chart improvement, and then set a date when you will review these priorities and adjust your plans if necessary.

I would like to improve in the following aspect of leading the instructional team:

_____

_____

I will take the following actions to bring about change:

_____

_____

_____

_____

_____

I will measure improvement or success in the following ways:

_____

_____

_____

_____

I will keep a record of what I do and changes I may see by doing the following:

_____

_____

_____

_____

_____

I will review progress toward this priority on this date: _____

Assigning Roles and Responsibilities

2

In the Introduction and Chapter 1, we stated that some responsibilities belong to the teacher alone, but others can—and should—be shared with the other adults who work in the classroom. An effective team approach in the classroom provides students with the best possible chance of success. In this chapter we discuss how you can prepare for and begin sharing classroom roles and responsibilities with your paraeducator. We help you to answer these questions:

- What is your role as the leader of the classroom instructional team?
- What responsibilities will you assign to your paraeducator?
- What exactly will you expect of your paraeducator with regard to each of those responsibilities?
- What other information do you need to give your paraeducator regarding her role and assignments?

Defining the Role of Classroom Instructional Team Leader

What is your role as the leader of the classroom instructional team? As a teacher, both tradition and policy govern what you do. In addition, the precise details of teachers' roles and responsibilities vary considerably from school to school—and even among classrooms. You may feel that you have a clear definition of what is expected of you in terms of responsibility for students, but you also need to consider your responsibilities in relation to your paraeducator. In essence, you need to define what your paraeducator can expect of you as leader of the classroom instructional team, in addition to what your students can expect of you, of your paraeducator, and of the interaction between the adults and the students in the classroom.

Figure 2.1 will help you to clarify both your own role and the roles you assign your paraeducator. First complete the top of the form: Responsibilities that are the teacher's alone. You might list such items as planning and modifying curriculum, organizing the daily teaching schedule, assigning grades for student work, meeting with parents, or selecting resource materials. The most important aspect of this exercise is not that your role should consist of a particular set of responsibilities, but rather that you understand your role so clearly that you can communicate to your paraeducator what she can expect of you and which areas are in your jurisdiction, not hers. Of course, among the responsibilities that you list for yourself is supervising your paraeducator.

As you compile this list of teacher responsibilities, consider why they are yours and not your paraeducator's. As a certified teacher, you have acquired knowledge and training that enable you to take charge of a classroom. You may be a relatively new teacher or a veteran with many years of experience; in either case, your certification and district or state requirements give you legal responsibility for the education of your students. The legal responsibility is an important point to remember as you assign responsibilities to your paraeducator and define the limits of those responsibilities.

Assigning Responsibilities to Your Paraeducator

What responsibilities will you assign to your paraeducator? The next portion of Figure 2.1 helps you to answer that question. List the specific responsibilities that you feel you can reasonably assign to your paraeducator (or that you already assign to her). Although you make the final decision as to your paraeducator's assignments, you may wish to discuss the list with her and let her know that you would like her input. You might give her a blank copy of the form and ask her to list her responsibilities and assignments as she understands them, and then compare your lists. She may base her list on the general job description used to hire her, which may not match the specifics of what you expect of her in the classroom. Keep an open mind as you discuss responsibilities and expectations. Make sure that your paraeducator understands that she can express her ideas and

Figure 2.1
TEACHER AND PARAEDUCATOR RESPONSIBILITIES

Responsibilities that are the teacher's alone

_____

_____

_____

_____

Responsibilities assigned to the paraeducator

Responsibility
Example: Assisting with reading

_____

_____

_____

_____

What does this include?
Example: Listening to students read, keeping records

_____

_____

_____

_____

What does this not include?
Example: Administering reading tests

_____

_____

_____

_____

opinions freely and without fear of being "corrected" or laughed at. Both of you may be surprised at the number of tasks the paraeducator lists.

During your discussion, remember the point made earlier. You are assigned as the teacher because of your training and qualifications. Your paraeducator has been hired to work under your supervision—whatever her qualifications. As the teacher, you have ultimate and legal responsibility for what happens in the classroom, and your primary responsibility is to ensure that your students have the best possible educational experience. As you assign and discuss roles and responsibilities with your paraeducator, you should therefore be considering her qualifications, training, and experience, and how those can be used to enhance your students' experience. This applies to the knowledge and expertise that she has—and does not have. If you are unsure whether you can assign certain responsibilities to her, check school and school district guidelines for restrictions regarding the employment of paraeducators.

In addition to asking her how she perceives her role, you might also ask your paraeducator if there are other assignments that she has not been given but that she believes she could take on. Remember to add information you may have gathered in Chapter 1 regarding her talents, travel experiences, or bilingual skills. For example, many paraeducators are members of the local community and may have experience as leaders in Girl Scouts or 4-H, as well as with their own children. On the other hand, if you feel that she does not have the expertise for a responsibility that you would like to give her or that she would like to take on, you should be sure that she receives the necessary training first. Do not list the responsibility as part of her role until she has the training and support to be successful. In later chapters we will discuss how you can assess your paraeducator's level of skills and knowledge and how you can provide on-the-job training so that you can expand or modify her responsibilities as her skills and knowledge increase.

If you work with more than one paraeducator, you will need to conduct this activity with each one separately. They may have similar roles, but will each have different strengths and levels of experience.

Determining What to Expect of Your Paraeducator

What exactly will you expect of your paraeducator with regard to each of the assigned responsibilities? The next phase of this role definition exercise will help you answer this question. The responsibilities you listed are probably quite general—for example, "helping students with math" or "assisting with behavior management." But what do these mean in everyday terms?

To be most effective, responsibilities need to be clearly defined, with specific instances given of both what the responsibility includes and what it does *not* include. For example, in some schools, paraeducators (and not teachers) are assigned to monitor students through "bus duty" and during playground activities. In many schools, only teachers (and not paraeducators) are expected to attend faculty meetings, back-to-school night, and parent-teacher conferences. Often the school administration makes these sorts of assignments, but within your classroom, as long as you follow the legal framework provided by the state and by the school and district administration, you have considerable freedom to assign and determine the extent of your paraeducator's roles. It is your duty to identify and correct serious misunderstandings about the extent of your paraeducator's responsibility and authority and to know the limitations that the school and the district place on responsibilities that can be assigned. This ensures that you all work within the bounds of the law and follow good safety practices. However, the important point is that you should be *very* explicit in communicating what you want—and do not want—your paraeducator to do. As you clarify your paraeducator's responsibilities, consider questions such as those in the following examples.

If you listed "help students with math," does that include correcting and giving grades for work completed, or does she only correct work but leave assignment of grades to you? Does it include showing the student how to do a math problem or procedure you've already explained? Does it include deciding when students can move on to another assignment?

If you listed "assist with behavior management," does that include correcting inappropriate student behavior while you are teaching, or should that wait until there is a break in the teaching process? Does it include giving rewards for appropriate behavior, or is that a teacher responsibility? Does it include sending students to "time out," or does she have to refer them to you? Does it include withdrawing student privileges, such as taking away recess time? Does it include taking a student out of the classroom for reprimands or calling a parent to report problems or misdeeds?

If you listed "work with groups of students during reading time," does that include deciding when students move on to a new basal reader? Does it include giving students homework assignments related to their reading? Does it include modifying classroom rules for when students are working in the group with her?

If you listed "helping out wherever she's needed," does that include sitting with just one child, or should she always move around and work with the whole class? Does it include organizing your desktop, desk drawers, and paperwork if she thinks they need it? Does it include starting the class on an activity if you're out of the room when the bell rings at the end of recess? Does it include meeting with other teachers or the attendance secretary to review absences?

Figure 2.1 (p. 14) includes space to make these clarifications for your paraeducator. It would be a good idea to work through this part of the form with her, so that she can ask questions and you can clarify your expectations.

Having redefined or clarified your paraeducator's responsibilities, you may find that you need to reconsider some of your established ways of working in the classroom. Did the discussion offer insights into better ways of working together and additional responsibilities you could appropriately assign? Had your paraeducator misunderstood what you expected of her? Did she provide you with insights about what she expects of you? Did you find areas of responsibility that you think you could share with your paraeducator? Shared decision making means shared ownership, a greater investment in the activity. It is much more motivating because each member of the team tries to find creative solutions to shared problems and challenges. As long as you stay within the legal limits set by the state, the school, and the district, you are free to share as much of your responsibility with your paraeducator as you and she feel comfortable with and can effectively accomplish.

Providing Additional Information to Your Paraeducator

What other information do you need to give your paraeducator regarding her role and assignments? All employees should know the expectations of their jobs. Knowing what is expected of you is important not only for classroom roles, but also for the school in general. Occasionally we all bump up against areas of our work in which we feel we need to register or resolve a complaint or concern. Usually these concerns can be taken care of at the school level, and the rule of thumb tends to be that if you want to resolve a problem, you go first to the source closest to that problem. In most cases in which a paraeducator is experiencing employment problems, the situation relates to a lack of understanding about what her role was specifically designed *not* to include and what she should *not* have done. But she may well have other sorts of concerns, and you can help her to avoid additional difficulties by providing her with information regarding such questions as the following:

• Whom does she go to if she has concerns about some of the things that you do as the classroom teacher and as her direct supervisor?

• What does she do and whom does she talk to if another teacher or member of the school staff is acting in a way that she feels is detrimental to a student or the school in general?

• Where does she go if her paycheck is inaccurate and she is underpaid or overpaid?

• Whom does she talk to about a pay raise or a change in responsibilities?

The importance of clarifying this issue of "chain of command" cannot be overemphasized. As a teacher you are probably well aware of your own line of command, but you cannot assume that your paraeducator will have the same sense of the school organization and of how things operate, particularly if she has not worked before or has worked in a different type of organization. In one case we are aware of, a paraeducator took her concerns about a student's education program directly to the school principal. She worked in a high school where the policy was that such concerns should be taken first to the teacher, then to the department head, and to the principal only if the concerns were still unresolved. The paraeducator was unaware of the policy and was fired for not following procedure! We hope that your paraeducator will not be subjected to such drastic measures, but you can help her to avoid even minor embarrassment and unnecessary difficulties by providing her with basic procedural information before difficulties arise. Support her by informing her that she should work to resolve problems at the point of concern—for example, with the student or with you, the teacher. And then offer her regular opportunities to talk about her work so that if she has concerns they can be resolved promptly.

As a teacher who works with a paraeducator, and particularly if you are her direct supervisor, you are in a position to be her advocate. In fact, you may be her only advocate. When paraeducators are hired for jobs for which they have little or no training, they may unknowingly be putting themselves in a vulnerable position. As the supervising teacher, you can assess the extent to which your paraeducator is adequately trained for her responsibilities. You are also in a position to provide most of the information and much of the training she needs. But if her training needs go beyond what you can reasonably provide in the classroom and during the course of your working day, you can be her advocate in approaching the school administration to request additional training. This sends a clear message—to your paraeducator and to the school administration—of the high value you place on training and on your paraeducator as a member of the classroom instructional team. It also emphasizes the importance you place on having your paraeducator working within legal and ethical limits.

Summary

Some classroom responsibilities belong to the teacher alone, whereas others can be shared. Within the legal limits imposed by your state and district, you need to consider which responsibilities must remain yours as a teacher and which ones you may share with your paraeducator or other adults who work with you. As you make the initial assignment of roles, you should carefully supervise your paraeducator's work so that you can be sure that you are not asking her to take on responsibilities for which she is not prepared. As she acquires more knowledge and skills, the two of you can expand her role to reflect the increased expertise. Assigning roles incrementally to correspond to your paraeducator's increasing skills is similar to the good instructional practices you use with your students—adding to their knowledge base after carefully determining that they have a sound understanding on which to build. These are good supervisory practices. They will ensure a better working relationship with your paraeducator, as you make clear your expectations of her and what she can expect from you. These practices will simplify classroom management as students see that both adults have consistent expectations, and they will contribute to an environment that optimizes student learning opportunities. Having more than one paraeducator on your instructional team will require additional clarification of responsibilities, but the effort will substantially strengthen the dynamics of the team.

In Practice

Following are some suggestions for ways in which you can apply what you have learned in this chapter to your own working situation. We also have provided space for you to add ideas that you glean from your experience and from interactions with colleagues.

• Ask your paraeducator if she has a job description—one that may have been given to her when she was hired. Often this is not the case; many paraeducators work without job descriptions. If she does not have one, ask the school administration if one exists or if the school has guidelines for responsibilities that may be assigned to paraeducators. If such guidelines exist, be sure to consider them when you define your paraeducator's responsibilities. If the school has no guidelines, you may wish to provide the school administration with a copy of the job description that you develop with your paraeducator.

• Find out if the school district or state has guidelines or job descriptions for paraeducators. You may also want to check with the special education department at the school district office, because some districts have done more to define roles for special education paraeducators.

• Refer to the activity in Chapter 1 in which you discussed or discovered your paraeducator's strengths and talents. See which of these can be incorporated into her classroom roles and responsibilities.

• _____

_____

_____

• _____

_____

_____

• _____

_____

_____

• _____

_____

_____

Setting Priorities for Improvement

Now that you have read the chapter on assigning roles and responsibilities and have had an opportunity to consider how this applies to the situation you work in, take some time to set priorities for your work in this area. Choose an aspect of assigning roles and responsibilities, list one or two ways in which you think you can improve in this area, decide how you will know if you have made improvements, determine ways in which you might keep a record and use it to chart improvement, and then set a date when you will review these priorities and adjust your plans if necessary.

I would like to improve in the following aspect of assigning roles and responsibilities:

_____

_____

I will take the following actions to bring about change:

_____

_____

_____

_____

_____

_____

I will measure improvement or success in the following ways:

_____

_____

_____

_____

I will keep a record of what I do and changes I may see by doing the following:

_____

_____

_____

_____

_____

I will review progress toward this priority on this date: _____

Improving Communications

3

In this chapter we analyze communications, looking at what makes communication more effective and the kinds of communication skills you can develop to enhance your effectiveness as a supervisor of paraeducators or other adults. We address these questions:

- What aspects of communication should you be aware of in your work with your paraeducator?
- How do you and your paraeducator approach your work, and why is it important to communicate about this?
- Do you make decisions based on principles or preferences?
- How can you use your paraeducator's strengths and preferences to help the two of you function more effectively as a team?
- How can you and your paraeducator use a problem-solving approach to making team decisions?

Understanding the Complexity of Communication

What aspects of communication should you be aware of in your work with your paraeducator? Before considering the answer to that question, take a moment to list some of the ways in which you now communicate with your paraeducator:

I communicate with my educator by _____

_____

_____

_____

_____

_____

Communication happens, intentionally and unintentionally. We are always communicating something to those around us. Look back at the list and note the ways in which you communicate. You may have included speaking, writing notes, gestures, facial expressions, and other body language. Most teachers know that often our most effective communication does not involve speech. But effective communication does mean conveying a message in such a way that the person you are communicating with understands it in the way you intended. We communicate with our students by standing next to them (as a reminder to get back to work) or by giving them "the look." A pat on the shoulder says "good job," and a smile says it all! If we do not communicate effectively, what we say may not be understood as we would like it to be, just as we may unknowingly misunderstand something that is said to us.

Here is an example. Think about this common statement: Children come to school to learn. What does it mean? What are children supposed to learn in school? Take a moment to write your thoughts on what this simple statement means to you.

Children come to school to learn. This statement means _____

_____

_____

_____

_____

_____

But what does this have to do with communication? Even a simple statement such as "Children come to school to learn" has a very different meaning depending on who is stating it. Everyone has different experiences, priorities, and approaches to life and work. Each person believes his or her meaning is "right," although there is no single right answer. Even in a very specific curriculum area, such as reading, the meaning can vary. Do children come to learn the alphabet? how to sound out letters? a love of books? cooperation and tolerance of others? social skills? All of these are important educational goals, but you may give them quite different priorities from another teacher, your paraeducator, or the child's parents. You may want to try asking other people this same question: What is it that children come to school to learn? Ask your paraeducator, a teenager, a five-year-old, and your mother. You will likely get very different answers.

The important point is that as a teacher you need to be aware that your paraeducator's mindset on how children learn and how classrooms are run may differ considerably from yours. You need to establish a common vocabulary and understanding on even the most common education phrases. You cannot assume that you are effectively communicating with her just because you tell her something in a way that you think is clear.

As the classroom teacher, your priorities will often take precedence, because you are responsible for what takes place and whether students learn. These priorities may not match those of your paraeducator, but if you make them clear, your paraeducator will have a better idea of what is expected of her and what she can expect of you. This is why we asked you in Chapter 2 to consider specific details of your role and of the responsibilities that you assign to your paraeducator.

Some authors (for example, Beebe, Beebe, & Redmond, 1999) have suggested that when two people interact or work together, they have to establish a common culture. Even if they come from the same ethnic background, they will each have a different personal culture because of family influences, life experiences, and personality. Effective collaboration and teamwork require them to establish a new culture for their work environment, one that they negotiate and agree to have in common and that will best serve the needs of their collaborative efforts. This third culture will contain elements from each of their personal cultures; they will both have to adapt some of their usual ways of working and adopt aspects of the other's culture that would not normally be part of their own. As you and your paraeducator clarify your expectations of each other, this is essentially what you are doing: negotiating a common culture for your working environment. It is within this common culture that your team will establish and communicate team goals.

This talk of a common culture is a good reminder that different cultures have very different ways of communicating, and that what is commonplace in one culture may be offensive in another. In some cultures the use of physical contact is more acceptable than in others. For a child to have eye contact with an adult is a sign of attention and respect among many people in the United States, ("Look at me when I'm talking to you, please"), but not among certain Asian groups, who show respect by averting the eyes. The use of first names among adults who work together is common in the United States, but not necessarily among people in many other cultures. We often use competition and gamesmanship to motivate students in schools in the United States; but for Navajo children, for example, succeeding as an individual is less important than helping the whole group to succeed, and so the use of competition becomes counterproductive. Likewise, for some cultures any comment made in public should be made quietly, and interrupting another person may be considered impolite; group discussions among people of those cultures have a very different feel compared with discussions held among people whose cultures accept lively exchanges and "heckling."

Your paraeducator's ethnic background may well be different from yours, but she may share the same ethnic background as many of your students. In terms of effective and acceptable ways of communicating, therefore, you may be able to take your lead from her, or ask her for suggestions and clarification on the best ways to communicate with your students and understand their thinking.

Communicating About Approaches to Work

How do you and your paraeducator approach your work, and why is it important to communicate about this? Clearly identifying your approach to your work and communicating this to other adults in your classroom gives you an opportunity to explore how you see your paraeducator's approach to her work and to clarify your impressions by discussing them with her.

Take time to outline the points that you want to emphasize as you communicate about classroom practices to your paraeducator. One teacher we know wanted to make certain her new paraeducator felt comfortable asking questions about the things she didn't understand, and so she said, "Just ask me any time you have a question." Later the paraeducator interrupted a math session in which the teacher was providing direct instruction to the students to ask about a classroom procedure. The teacher was amazed that the paraeducator did not know that she was not to interrupt a teaching session, but what had she said? Thinking carefully about your expectations can prevent problems by reducing chances of your assuming that your paraeducator will know something when in fact she has not been trained or taught the concept.

Among the things that drive the way in which we respond to events are our beliefs or principles. Much has been written about beliefs, principles, and values, and we discuss this in more detail later; but let it suffice here to say that what we believe influences how we respond to situations. For example, one person may find a dollar on the sidewalk, pick it up, and search all day to find the "rightful owner"—the one who lost the dollar. Another person may find a dollar on the sidewalk, pick it up, put it in a pocket, and say, "Finders keepers, losers weepers." These two people would be at odds with each other if they were to discuss who is "right" in this situation, because each operates under a different set of principles. In the same way, conflict can arise in a classroom setting when people who have different principles work in the same space.

Figure 3.1 (p. 30) can help you and your paraeducator clarify classroom and instructional issues (and identify possible differences in principles) and begin communication about potential conflicts. Figure 3.1 lists some issues related to working in the classroom and asks you to state how you feel about each one. Check one of the options listed underneath each issue on the left side of the page. On the right side of the page you are asked to state how you have communicated your feelings about these issues to your paraeducator. You may have difficulty completing this part of the form. If so, this is a good indication that you need to take the time to consider how you could communicate your feelings so that there is no misunderstanding between you and your paraeducator.

A second version of the form (Figure 3.2, p. 31) lists the same issues, but asks you to answer according to what you think your paraeducator's feelings are and to state how she has communicated this to you. Again, check one of the options on the left, and then in the space on the right give examples of how your paraeducator has communicated her preferences to you. You might give your paraeducator the same forms to complete, having her substitute the word *teacher* for *paraeducator*. In that case, she will be able to state her preferences and how she has communicated them to you, and then state what she thinks your preferences are and how you have communicated them to her. If you ask her to complete the forms, you can either exchange them or—better still—sit down together and compare what each of you has written about how you perceive each other's preferences. You may have identified those preferences quite accurately, or you may find considerable discrepancies. In either case, the exercise will certainly have clarified a number of important classroom issues for both of you.

Making Decisions Based on Principles or Preferences

Do you make decisions based on principles or preferences? One way to look at the daily decisions that you make and communicate to others is to ask yourself whether *principle* or *preference* is involved. Think about the difference between these two things. A *principle* is something by which you govern your life—a truth, law, or moral standard that you believe in and that governs your conduct. Principles relate to ethics and how you think things "should" be done. It is generally considered a matter of integrity not to compromise your principles. A *preference* has more to do with likes and dislikes—things you prefer but that are not mandatory. Although you may have a strong preference for having things done in a particular way, you are more likely to negotiate and cede to someone else's preferences than you are to compromise your principles.

Take a moment to list some of the things that you consider to be principles and preferences.

Principles   **_Preferences_**

_____   _____
_____   _____
_____   _____
_____   _____
_____   _____
_____   _____
_____   _____

Let's look at an example that shows why it is important to make this distinction. Among the people you work with there are probably some who are never late. You may be one of them. These people feel that they must always be on time as a matter of principle—they believe it shows respect for other people's time and efforts and it contributes to their efficiency. They work very hard to keep to that standard. Other people you work with may prefer to be on time, but if something else that they consider to be more important comes up, they are not upset by the thought of being 10 minutes late for a meeting. And, of course, other people among your colleagues never seem to know what time it is and seem to be totally oblivious to whether they or anyone else is punctual or not.

The conflict arises when the person functioning on principle has a meeting scheduled with the person functioning on preference or the person who has no sense of time at all. The first person may consider the second unreasonable and rude: "Why is it so difficult to expect someone to turn up on time? Doesn't she think I have better things to do than wait for her?" The other person may think that living by the clock is rigid and unreasonable. They are at odds with each other, neither understanding the other's perspective or being willing to cede.

Sometimes interpersonal communication is poor because we have not conveyed the reasoning behind why we do certain things. Self-evaluation is important to help you determine whether you are doing things because of principle or preference. Once you have decided _why_ you do what you do, you can then

Figure 3.1
COMMUNICATING PREFERENCES: THE TEACHER'S PERSPECTIVE

How do I feel about . . . ?

Punctuality
____ It's not something I really think about.
____ I prefer it, but it's not a priority.
____ It's a priority.

Taking initiative
____ I enjoy other people's creativity.
____ I encourage and consider suggestions.
____ I don't like surprises.

Close supervision
____ As the person responsible, the teacher needs to be in control.
____ I like my personal space, but I also like working collaboratively.
____ Mature adults shouldn't need close supervision.

The working environment
____ It's impossible to be efficient if the classroom is untidy.
____ A little clutter is inevitable in the classroom, and that's OK.
____ Clutter? What clutter?!

What have I done to let my paraeducator know that this is how I feel?

_____

_____

_____

_____

_____

_____

_____

_____

_____

Figure 3.2
COMMUNICATING PREFERENCES: THE PARAEDUCATOR'S PERSPECTIVE

How do I think my paraeducator feels about . . .?

Punctuality
____ It's not something she really thinks about.
____ She prefers it, but it's not a priority.
____ It's a priority for her.

Taking initiative
____ She enjoys being creative and taking initiative.
____ She knows that she can make suggestions.
____ She wouldn't do anything without my permission.

Close supervision
____ As the person responsible, the teacher needs to be in control.
____ She likes her personal space but also likes collaborative work.
____ She doesn't feel that she needs close supervision.

The working environment
____ It's impossible to be efficient if the classroom is untidy.
____ A little clutter is inevitable in the classroom, and that's OK.
____ Clutter? What clutter?!

How do I know? (What has she done to communicate this to me?)

_____

_____

_____

_____

_____

_____

_____

_____

_____

communicate this to the adults you are working with. For example, you may choose words like "I make it a rule to arrive for faculty meetings on time because I feel it's discourteous to keep other people waiting"; then you can discuss with your paraeducator what this means in terms of classroom action. You might discuss, for example, what she could do to help if a parent showed up to talk about a problem just before a faculty meeting is to begin.

It is estimated that on average about 14 percent of every 40-hour work week (or more than one whole morning of school) is wasted because of poor interpersonal communication. What can be done about it? Two things come to mind.

First, consider the items that you previously listed as principles or preferences. On what grounds, if any, would you be prepared to concede any of your principles? Take the example of punctuality again. Ask yourself these questions:

• Are there any circumstances under which lack of punctuality (in another person or in yourself) would be acceptable? What would those circumstances be?

• Would a simple explanation from the other person help you to accept what they had done?

Remember the point made earlier: Make your expectations clear; give examples of what you mean and of the circumstances under which certain things are acceptable or not acceptable; do not leave your paraeducator guessing. Consider the above questions for each of the items that you have listed as principles. If you can think of any reasonable grounds for "compromising" any of the principles, they may just be strong preferences. Even if you still consider them to be principles, this leads to the second point.

When someone violates what you consider to be a principle, reserve judgment about why they may be doing it, and do what you can to discover the reason behind their choice. A familiar scenario for anyone who drives is the sign that indicates that one of the lanes will be closed a quarter of a mile ahead. You pull over into the lane that will remain open, not wishing to have to squeeze into the fast-moving traffic at the last minute. However, as you continue driving—at reduced speed now that most of the traffic is in one lane—you see several cars speeding past in the lane that is soon to be closed. You know that they will further reduce your speed as they push their way into "your" lane at the last minute. Does this sound familiar? What are your thoughts as you see those cars speed by? Do you think, "Those jerks! Didn't they see the sign? They should have pulled over, as I did. Why should I let them squeeze in front of me?" Or do you think, "There must be a good reason for them to be in such a hurry. Perhaps they are rushing to the hospital because their child is sick."

Realistically, in the scene just described, most of the drivers who speed past and squeeze in at the last minute do not have a sick child or an emergency to deal with. And this may be true of much of the behavior that you find unacceptable in colleagues or students. The important point to remember is that you decide what motives you ascribe to the actions of others. If you want to enhance the effectiveness of your communication—and therefore your relationship—with your paraeducator, you must reserve judgment and seek clarification on why things are done in a particular way, so that in turn you can clarify your expectations about how you would *prefer* to have things done.

Making Good Use of Your Paraeducator's Strengths and Preferences

How can you use your paraeducator's strengths and preferences to help the two of you function more effectively as a team? Having decided what your preferred work style is and which things you do out of principle and which you do because of preference, the next important thing to consider is how this affects your work with your paraeducator. No one style or approach is intrinsically better than another—each has its strengths and weaknesses. What makes them effective is how we use them in different situations.

We often use a different style or approach instinctively in different situations or with different people, knowing that someone will respond better to a particular approach; in other words, we make use of the strengths of another communication style. We do this with the adults we work with and with our students, and we do it because it works. We know that the adult or child we are trying to communicate with will respond better to a different approach, will appreciate a different type of reasoning or argument, and will understand what is required much better if we rephrase and tackle the problem from a different angle.

Take a moment to consider how you approach your work with your paraeducator and how you adapt to her preferred style of communication or approach to her work. List three things that you already do—or that you could do—to communicate more effectively with your paraeducator. Then note why you do each of the things you've listed. We've given you an example to start you off.

Example: Write a list of daily tasks—she seems to forget unless it's written down.

1. _____

_____

2. _____

_____

3. _____

_____

Now list three things that your paraeducator does for you (or that you would really like her to do for you) to communicate more effectively. Again, it would be a good idea to say why you like these things, and we have given you an example.

Example: She asks for an explanation when she doesn't understand—I sometimes forget to give details of what I want done, and it's a good reminder for me to be more explicit.

1. _____

_____

2. _____

_____

3. _____

_____

Identifying some of the things that you do to enhance communication with your paraeducator should serve as a reminder to continue doing those things. If your list contains things that you could do but have not yet initiated, this should prompt you to start doing those things. Having identified some of the things that your paraeducator does for you, you might let her know that you appreciate her consideration for your preferences. If the second list contains items that you would like her to do, take the time to sit down with her and make some simple requests. Remember to ask her if there are other things that she would like you to do for her to enhance communication between you.

Using a Problem-Solving Approach

How can you and your paraeducator use a problem-solving approach to making team decisions? Difficult and frustrating situations can arise in your work, and it is often a challenge to see these situations objectively. Figure 3.3 provides a way in which you can look more objectively at problems that may arise and work through them systematically. The act of writing down how you see a situation and generating solutions on paper requires that you stop and think before you make any decisions. If your paraeducator is involved in the situation, give her a copy of the form to complete and then meet to discuss her perspective and suggestions and to share your viewpoint and ideas with her.

The first part of Figure 3.3 asks you to describe the situation. When you do this, state the facts and try to avoid making judgmental statements, although you can include feelings. If the situation makes you frustrated or angry, for example, you can include that fact in your description. Next the form asks you to decide whether the situation concerns a matter of principle or preference. Circle the one that applies. Then list some suggestions for what could be done to improve the situation. Treat this as a brainstorming opportunity rather than a list of final decisions about what action to take. Next to each suggestion write the name of the

Figure 3.3
A PROBLEM-SOLVING TEMPLATE FOR ENHANCED COMMUNICATION

1. What is happening? (Briefly describe the situation.)

_____

_____

_____

_____

2. This is a matter of (circle one):   principle   preference

3. What could be done to make the situation better?
(List as many things as you can think of.)

_____

_____

_____

_____

4. Who should take responsibility for these things? (If you have not already
done so, next to each of the items listed in #3, write the name of the person
who you think should take responsibility for the action—you, your
paraeducator, a school administrator, etc.)

5. Realistically, how much of a problem is this? (Check one.)

☐ This is a relatively minor problem, but changes do need to be made.
☐ This is a major problem and needs immediate attention.

6. What will you do to start resolving the situation?

_____

_____

_____

_____

person whose responsibility that action should be. If you have already stated this in your suggestions, underline the name or title of the person. If the list contains suggestions of things that other people should be doing to resolve the problem and your name does not appear next to any of the suggestions, this is a good indication that you should add some things that you could do. Likewise, if all of the suggestions have your name next to them, take this as a hint that you do not need to take all of the responsibility yourself and generate some suggestions for actions that you might ask other people to take. Question 5 asks you to assess how much of a problem this situation really represents, in light of your objective description and the actions you have listed. The last question asks you to state at least one thing that you will do to start resolving the situation.

Use this process of objectively writing down your thoughts and ideas whenever a situation arises that causes you concern and for which you feel you need someone else's insights. Your paraeducator may be the ideal person because she is well acquainted with your students and classroom routines and should be able to offer a slightly different perspective. Even if the situation involves a difficulty with your paraeducator, you can use this form to make the problem-solving process more objective.

Summary

If you have completed all of the activities suggested in this chapter, you should have a clearer understanding of the complexity of communication and why good communication is important to your successful work with your paraeducator. Through self-evaluation you should have identified your approach to work, the preferences of your paraeducator, and therefore the ways in which you can work more effectively with her. You should also be more aware of your own communication preferences and what you have already done to enhance communication in your classroom. You can save valuable instructional time and prevent hurt or angry feelings by talking to your paraeducator about how she sees her work and yours, the way in which she likes to approach the tasks that are assigned to her, and the value that she assigns to different aspects of classroom procedures and practices. Do what you can to discover what her preferences are and the principles that govern her behavior. Encourage her to let you know her preferences and principles while letting her know yours. Be creative in finding ways to communicate if it is hard to find time for face-to-face communication. When you are meeting and discussing issues, ascribe positive motives to actions you are unsure of, and then discuss and resolve them.

In Practice

Following are some suggestions for applying what you have learned in this chapter to your own working situation. We also have provided space for you to add ideas that you glean from your own experience and interactions with colleagues.

• Type up a list of standard classroom procedures and keep the list in a three-ring binder in an easily accessible location so that your paraeducator can always check anything she is unsure of. The binder can also be available to anyone else who comes into the classroom and needs to know procedures, such as student teachers or volunteers. This reference can reduce the number of instructions you have to give orally and minimizes interruptions.

• If your paraeducator does not have a mailbox in the school, offer to put her name on yours and let the secretarial or administrative staff know so that they can direct relevant materials to her via your mailbox.

• Ask your paraeducator, "If there were one thing that you could change about the classroom, what would it be and why?" Then act upon her suggestion. Even making a small change in procedures can make a big difference in how well the classroom functions, and your paraeducator may have many helpful suggestions for such small changes. Have the courage to ask that question periodically and see what results it brings. You can ask yourself the same question, and if you identify something that you'd like to change but don't know how, ask your paraeducator's advice on that, too.

• Create an opportunity to discuss different approaches and communication styles with your students. Ask them if they see differences in the way your paraeducator works with them and the way you work with them. Help them to see that these different approaches bring variety and interest to the class. This will be an important lesson for them to learn—that there are many ways of approaching a task, each with its own merits—and it will serve as a reminder to you of the rich diversity among your students that you need to accommodate as you also use that diversity as a bonus in the classroom.

- _____

_____

_____

- _____

_____

_____

- _____

_____

_____

Setting Priorities for Improvement

Now that you have read about improving communications and have had an opportunity to consider how this applies to the situation you work in, take some time to set priorities for your work in this area. Choose an aspect of communication, list one or two ways in which you think you can improve in this area, decide how you will know if you have made improvements, determine ways in which you might keep a record and use it to chart improvement, and then set a date when you will review these priorities and adjust your plans if necessary.

I would like to improve in the following aspect of communication:

_____

_____

I will take the following actions to bring about change:

_____

_____

_____

_____

_____

_____

I will measure improvement or success in the following ways:

_____

_____

_____

_____

I will keep a record of what I do and changes I may see by doing the following:

_____

_____

_____

_____

_____

I will review progress toward this priority on this date: _____

Monitoring the Quality of Your Paraeducator's Work

4

Whether they call it evaluating, assessing, checking, or just "keeping an eye on things," monitoring classroom activities and behavior is something all teachers do. In fact, more effective teachers do it more often than less effective teachers. In classrooms that are well managed, teacher-managers constantly monitor what is going on so that they can take preventive measures and have fewer problems and disruptions. In this chapter we address these questions:

• Why is student behavior and progress monitored, and is paraeducators' work monitored for the same reasons?

• How can you establish monitoring your paraeducator as a positive and supportive procedure designed to assist her in her work?

• How can you teach your paraeducator to monitor her own work?

The Reasons for Monitoring

Why is student behavior and progress monitored, and is paraeducators' work monitored for the same reasons? Some teachers and paraeducators who are assigned to the same classroom tell us that they do not watch each other—as if they fear that there may be an implied criticism in admitting that they observe someone else's work. We find it hard to believe that this can be so, but think for a moment about why you monitor your students' work and behavior. Write down some of the things that you monitor in your classroom, and why you monitor those things.

I monitor . . .	*because . . .*
_____	_____
_____	_____
_____	_____
_____	_____
_____	_____

As a teacher, a large proportion of your time is spent on these forms of monitoring:

- Checking on what students are doing and how well they are doing it
- Assessing how well classroom procedures and organization are working
- Evaluating the effectiveness of the instruction you provide according to the reactions and progress of your students
- Checking to see whether students retain the information later

Some of the monitoring you do is formal (you may give an end-of-unit test to monitor student understanding), but much of it is informal (you watch for evidence of students being distracted or off-task as they change activities or work independently). Whatever form it takes, monitoring is something an effective teacher does frequently. Monitoring allows you to keep control of the classroom in a general sense, but on a much more important level it allows you to continually make adjustments in what you do and how you do it, so that students get the maximum benefit from their classroom experiences.

In classroom or action research terms, we would say that you are collecting data in order to make data-based decisions about the effectiveness of your teaching. This is true even when the research is not formalized and the data is not written down. You notice what students do in response to your teaching and make a note (albeit a mental one) to remember that a particular strategy was successful or to try a slightly different approach because the strategy was not successful. You see that something works with a particular student or group of students and make a note to try the same thing with others. This is effective classroom practice, and the more carefully and often you monitor what is going on, the better able you will be to accommodate students' needs and maximize their learning opportunities. Good teachers are good monitors and adjusters of classroom interactions.

Now think about monitoring your paraeducator and her work. List in the left-hand column below the ways in which you monitor your paraeducator. (List *how* you monitor, not *what* you monitor. For example, you may watch from a distance as she teaches or have her keep a list of the activities she completes with the students each day.) Then write in the right-hand column why you do this.

*I monitor my paraeducator
in these ways . . .*   *because . . .*

_____   _____
_____   _____
_____   _____
_____   _____
_____   _____
_____   _____

Your list probably included such items as watching her as she works, talking to her about her work, having her keep a record of things she does during the day, or completing an annual evaluation. And the main reason you do this is surely the same as the reason for monitoring your students and their work: you want to be sure that the students gain the greatest possible benefit from their classroom experience. Because your paraeducator is part of that experience, it is your responsibility as a teacher to monitor her classroom practices. She stands in for you as a partner in the instructional process; she is in a sense one of the tools you use to provide instruction for students. And that means that monitoring is a vital activity for an effective supervisor of paraeducators.

Although most teachers monitor their paraeducator in some way, many of them don't know what to do about what they observe. We will cover that topic in the next chapters, with suggestions on how you can help your paraeducator to increase her skills and effectiveness. First, however, we will consider some of the practicalities of monitoring your paraeducator's work.

Making Monitoring Positive and Supportive

How can you establish monitoring your paraeducator as a positive and supportive procedure designed to assist her in her work? We mentioned earlier that many teachers and paraeducators tell us that they never watch each other in the classroom. Teachers seem to feel that there is a negative connotation to observing their paraeducator's work—as if it implies that they cannot trust the paraeducator to work unsupervised, or as if they are obliged to look for faults and shortcomings. Paraeducators seem to feel that what the teacher does is not their business and that it is not their place to "keep an eye" on the teacher. The more likely scenario is that teachers and paraeducators both watch each other fairly extensively—which makes good sense, because much can be gained from doing so. We encourage and recommend joint monitoring and believe that the first step toward establishing it as a positive and supportive procedure is to admit to it and make it a deliberate part of the classroom routine. Here are some suggestions. (More suggestions appear in the "In Practice" section at the end of the chapter.)

• Establish the habit of teaching near each other. Work with the same group of students on a regular basis so that you each see what the other is doing and hear each other's responses to student questions. Having your paraeducator work in close physical proximity to you is a first step toward "giving her permission" to watch what you do as a teacher.

• Teach a lesson with your paraeducator. Discuss the lesson that you will teach together and decide which parts of it you will each present. Do not go away and do something else while your paraeducator is teaching her assigned portions; sit among the students and have her do the same while you are teaching your assigned segments. Again, this establishes watching and monitoring each other as a legitimate classroom practice. Do be sure that she has the necessary skills before assigning her segments to teach.

• Tell your paraeducator that you have been watching her work and compliment her on her skills. She knows that you watch her anyway, so you might as well be honest about it and use it as an opportunity to recognize the contribution she makes in the classroom.

• Ask her to monitor the students' work and behavior and to let you know if she has concerns. Let her know that this type of continuous informal assessment of the classroom environment is important in helping you (and her) to know what is happening and to make adjustments as necessary; if she observes reactions from the students to things that you do, particularly things that perhaps you would not have noticed yourself, she should also let you know, so that you can both become more aware of the effects your teaching is having on the students.

• Ask her opinion of the effectiveness of some of the things you do, making the connection between your behavior and the effect it has on the students. You might begin the conversation by saying something like this:

> I've been trying to give more students an opportunity to express their opinions by setting up the weekly debating session. You've been in the classroom when we've done that. How do you think it's working? Do you think enough of the students are having a say? Or is it still the same ones who always talk? How can we get more of them to join in?

Encourage her to make suggestions—and then act upon them to show that you value her opinion.

These are just a few of the things that you can do to legitimize the process of adults monitoring each other's practice in your classroom. Make it an overt and frequent practice, and it will become an asset to your teamwork. It should also help to make your communication more effective as you become accustomed to exchanging ideas on what you have observed each other doing.

Teaching Your Paraeducator to Self-Monitor

How can you teach your paraeducator to monitor her own work? To begin with, you should discuss with your paraeducator the importance of monitoring one's own work. The first step in this process is to make more obvious the fact that you monitor your own work. Much of your monitoring, as we have already stated, is probably informal, and much of it takes place in your head—the process is not apparent to someone who is observing you. For this reason you need to make it a visible process for your paraeducator. If you want to emphasize the importance of recording useful things that she sees—in relation to what you do (and what she should therefore do herself) or what the students do—you will need to both encourage her to keep a record and provide her with the necessary materials. Offer her a three-ring binder or a simple journal-type book, show her your own records (even if they are just scribblings), and check with her periodically to see what useful things she has learned and might like to share with you. Encourage her to record activities or approaches that she used with the students that worked (her successes) as well as those things that did not seem to be effective (what she might consider failures) and offer to discuss both with her. You can both learn from each other's successes and failures. Remember to share yours with her—the days when things went wrong as well as when they went right—so that she knows that she is not the only adult learner in the classroom.

In Chapter 5 we discuss observation as a first step toward providing training for your paraeducator and provide a simple form for recording observations. Here are some other methods that you could suggest to your paraeducator for recording observations made during classroom interactions:

• A simple journal or running record with the date and a brief note about what she saw or learned

• A card index with topic headings for subject areas (reading, math, artwork) or aspects of her work (organizing group work, keeping students on task, rewarding good behavior), under which she can file cards with notes about things she did herself or saw you do that worked well, or ideas that she would like to try

• A small notebook or a clipboard that she can carry with her or that is readily available at her work station, so that she can make brief notes as interesting events occur

You may wish to point out to your paraeducator that the things she records do not need to be major events or particularly unusual. Many of the items that you automatically note and store for future use are probably simple and unexceptional. But taken together, all of the pieces of information provide you with what you need to make informed choices and judgments about the effectiveness of your teaching and adjustments that you might need to make.

Summary

Monitoring classroom interactions is an important part of being an effective educator. This applies to your role as an instructor and to your role as supervisor of a paraeducator or other adults in the classroom. You use many different means of collecting information about your students—from informal observations to formal standardized tests—in order to enhance their learning experiences. Similarly, you use several methods of monitoring your paraeducator's work, although they are not likely to be formalized, for the same purpose: ensuring that your students are provided with the best possible learning opportunities and experiences. It makes good sense to watch what others do in order to learn from them, and if you wish to be a more effective supervisor, you need to openly discuss and encourage monitoring of each other's work as a type of mutual learning among the adults in your classroom.

In Practice

Following are some suggestions for ways in which you can apply what you have learned in this chapter to your own work situation. We also have provided space for you to add ideas that you glean from your own experience and interactions with colleagues.

• Be sure you have a clear idea of what you want to accomplish before you ask your paraeducator to observe your instruction. Explain clearly the things you want her to watch for so that she can gain from her observations.

• Your paraeducator is a valuable member of the instructional team. Demonstrate to her that you value her contributions by monitoring and observing her work, acknowledging the skills she has, and providing feedback to her on what she has accomplished.

• Take time to communicate your learning objectives for students to your paraeducator, and model the techniques you use to help achieve those objectives.

• _____

_____

_____

• _____

_____

_____

• _____

_____

_____

Setting Priorities for Improvement

Now that you have read the chapter on monitoring your paraeducator's work and have had an opportunity to consider how this applies to the situation you work in, take some time to set priorities for your work in this area. Choose an aspect of monitoring your paraeducator's work, list one or two ways in which you think you can improve in this area, decide how you will know if you have made improvements, determine ways in which you might keep a record and use it to chart improvement, and then set a date when you will review these priorities and adjust your plans if necessary.

I would like to improve in the following aspect of monitoring my paraeducator's work:

_____

_____

I will take the following actions to bring about change:

_____

_____

_____

_____

_____

I will measure improvement or success in the following ways:

_____

_____

_____

_____

I will keep a record of what I do and changes I may see by doing the following:

_____

_____

_____

_____

I will review progress toward this priority on this date: _____

Providing On-the-Job Training 5

You, as a teacher, can provide on-the-job training for your paraeducator in many ways. In this chapter we briefly discuss the importance of how you approach this training with another adult, as compared with the training or teaching you provide to your students, and suggest some resources that are likely to be available to you but that you may not be sharing with your paraeducator. The remainder of the chapter describes a training procedure that you can use to maximize the learning that takes place as you work alongside each other and she sees your example of how to be an effective educator. These are the specific questions that we address:

• How can you be sure that you treat your paraeducator appropriately as an adult learner?

• How can you enable your paraeducator to benefit from the professional organizations and publications that you have access to?

• How can you maximize the effect of the role model that you provide for your paraeducator?

Treating Your Paraeducator as an Adult Learner

How can you be sure that you treat your paraeducator appropriately as an adult learner? As an adult, your paraeducator will have some similarities but many differences in her learning needs as compared with your students. Take a moment to consider some of these differences and similarities. Listed below are some statements that describe younger students. Under the column headed "Adult Learners," write a possible corresponding characteristic.

Younger Students	*Adult Learners*
They have limited life experience to draw upon.	_____ _____
They are largely dependent upon adults for guidance and knowledge.	_____ _____
They are in school because of a legal requirement to attend (although we hope they also want to be there).	_____ _____ _____
They may still be at a fact-finding stage of learning.	_____ _____
Learning is their "work"—they know they are expected to study, read, and write.	_____ _____ _____

Your paraeducator, as an adult learner, has a wealth of experience and knowledge, even though that experience and knowledge may not be in education or be related to children. She is probably accustomed to being independent and making her own decisions and will have some definite ideas about what she values and respects, as well as how she expects to be treated. Her learning interests are most likely to be of a problem-solving nature, and she seeks answers to the questions she has about her work. In many of these ways she is quite different from your students, although as students move into the higher grade levels, we would hope that they are learning to be more independent, to be better problem solvers, and to gain insight into life experiences.

Add to these differences the possibility that your paraeducator may be older than you and may have more experience both in the classroom and with children and you can see that "educating" your paraeducator requires quite a different approach in many ways than educating young students. However, there are similarities. Think of some of the similarities that exist—both in the learning needs of paraeducators and students and in the approach that you can use.

Similarities: Both paraeducators and students . . .

_____

_____

_____

_____

_____

One of the most important similarities is that effective instructional practices will help both paraeducators and students to learn. With this in mind, we offer the following suggestions:

• You should always check if your paraeducator has the necessary skills before making assignments that require use of those skills; if you are not sure, give an assignment that requires a fairly low level of the skill and watch to see how well she does before assigning work that requires a higher level of that skill.

• Monitor your paraeducator's work regularly; watch how she interacts with students, how well she manages student behavior, and how confident and competent she is in providing instruction to students or in any other task assigned to her. We discussed monitoring your paraeducator's work at some length in Chapter 4, so you are already familiar with the reasons for monitoring and the various ways you can accomplish it.

• Work with your paraeducator to provide her with new opportunities to learn that are relevant to her work and that match her preferred learning style and capabilities.

• Provide your paraeducator with many opportunities to practice new skills— first under your direction and mentoring and then independently.

• Establish a working environment in which asking questions is encouraged, where no question is too foolish, and where you model the importance of questioning how effective your work is and taking steps to improve.

You will recognize these practices as part of your repertoire as a teacher of students. They will also stand you in good stead as a teacher of adults.

In addition, assume that your paraeducator wants to learn and improve; assume that she will learn more easily and willingly if she receives encouragement and recognition for her efforts; assume that she will work more confidently and well if she knows exactly what is expected of her and knows that she has your support. These are assumptions that you make about your students that validate your work as an educator.

Making Professional Resources Accessible

How can you enable your paraeducator to benefit from the professional organizations and publications that you have access to? Our research suggests that the majority of paraeducators generally do not belong to professional organizations, nor do they access the education magazines and journals that these professional organizations produce. This is often true even if the teachers they work with belong to these organizations and subscribe to publications and the school in which they work carries subscriptions to publications on behalf of the faculty. It suggests that paraeducators are not aware that membership is available to them or that the school has publications that they can use to help them do their work more easily and effectively.

Several professional organizations are now actively recruiting paraprofessional staff. These include the National Education Association (NEA) and the American Federation of Teachers (AFT), as well as the Council for Exceptional Children (CEC) and organizations for classified staff or public school employees. In recognition of paraeducators' modest pay, these organizations often provide reduced membership rates. A growing number of states also produce newsletters and hold statewide training conferences specifically for paraeducators. Your paraeducator may not know about these. So what can you do? Here are some suggestions.

- As you read your own education publications, make a note of items that would be useful to your paraeducator. Be sure that they are at the right level of understanding and match what you expect her to do, and make it clear that you would like her not only to read the item but also to talk to you about it afterward, so that you can clarify points that she may not have understood and relate what she has read to her work.

- Let your paraeducator know about the journals and magazines that the school subscribes to, where they are kept, and that she may read them.

- Provide your paraeducator with information about membership in any of the professional organizations that you think would be appropriate and useful for her, and any publications you come across that would be helpful. You will find membership information and Web site addresses for several of the larger professional organizations in the References and Resources section at the end of this book.

- Talk to the principal at your school, the secretarial staff, or anyone else who is likely to receive information about paraeducator conferences, training, or publications, and ask that a copy of relevant materials be routed to your paraeducator's mailbox, or yours if she does not have one. Even better, arrange for her to have her own mailbox if possible, so that she can receive relevant items directly and without feeling that she may be invading your privacy.

All of these activities are aimed at helping your paraeducator gain access to information that will help her to do her job better; many of the materials will provide information on effective teaching techniques and will be helpful resources in providing training. Perhaps it will also help you as a teacher to know that you do not have to carry the entire responsibility for providing training for each new paraeducator who comes your way.

Maximizing the Role Model Effect

How can you maximize the effect of the role model that you provide for your paraeducator? As a teacher you are constantly working in front of an "audience": your students watch what you do and so do the other adults you work with. Some students and adults are more observant than others and will notice more details; others are less observant (or perhaps less curious) and do not as readily pick up on the details. You know that your students differ in this respect: some of them will notice what you do and readily adapt their behavior to your standards or preferences; others need to have standards of behavior and procedural preferences clearly explained and interpreted for them. We have already discussed the importance of making expectations clear in previous chapters. Here we discuss how you can make the example and role model that you provide for your paraeducator more obvious and instructive, and how you can provide your paraeducator with a vocabulary for the techniques you use.

What we propose here is a peer-mediated self-evaluation procedure that you can use both to train your paraeducator and to improve your own effectiveness. This procedure is based upon the principles of effective instruction in that it follows these four steps:

1. Model a skill or behavior that you want your paraeducator to master or improve while your paraeducator observes you.

2. Direct her observation and focus it on the critical features of the skill or behavior while you ask her to collect data on what she sees you do.

3. Look at the data she has collected, use it to make a self-evaluation of your own effectiveness, and discuss with your paraeducator how she can also use the information to improve her teaching.

4. Have her practice using the skill as you observe her, taking data that she can use to make a self-evaluation and discuss the implications of the data with her afterward.

Many teachers use modeling to teach their paraeducator instructional or other classroom skills. However, it is not sufficient or particularly effective to tell your paraeducator merely to "Watch how I teach" or "I want you to use the same behavior management procedures that I do." If you do this, you leave too much to chance and risk having to constantly correct misinterpretations. You will greatly enhance the chances of your paraeducator learning from the role model you provide by adding to the "Watch what I do . . ." some specifics, such as "Watch for the questions I ask" or "Watch the way I recognize appropriate behavior" and asking your paraeducator to record exactly what she sees. Direct her attention to a very specific aspect of teaching that is so well defined that there is no chance of misunderstanding, and small enough for her to tackle immediately in her own work.

Figure 5.1 shows a sample observation form to use for this purpose. Although you could use a plain piece of paper, using a form such as this one formalizes the process and helps you keep a more accurate and complete record of when you have provided training for your paraeducator. It also shows that you think this activity is important. You might provide your paraeducator with a three-ring binder to keep these forms in so that she has a record of the observations you have conducted. Let's consider an example.

Mrs. Parry is a paraeducator in Miss Tina's class. Miss Tina has asked Mrs. Parry to read with a small group of her 6th grade students. These students can read fairly well, but Miss Tina would like to encourage them to think more about what they are reading. She believes a group discussion will help. Mrs. Parry has read with students before but always in the lower grades where they were still struggling with the basic skills, and mostly with individual students rather than groups. However, she is willing to try. They talk about ways in which they can make the students think more about their reading, and Mrs. Parry seems to feel comfortable with asking questions to provoke thinking. Miss Tina says that she wants to be sure that the students have a good grasp of the facts as well, which means that the questions need to address the facts of the stories as well as make the students analyze those facts in some way. Miss Tina suggests that Mrs. Parry observe her as she works with the group of students and that she use an observation form (such as the one we have provided) to write down all of the questions that Miss Tina asks. They can get together afterward to talk about what Mrs. Parry has written on the form.

Figure 5.1
OBSERVATION FORM

Date: _____   Time: _____

Current Area of Focus:

Observations: Notes:

Possible Next Area of Focus:

They conduct the discussion group and observation while the rest of the class is working independently on an assignment, and Mrs. Parry presents the completed form to Miss Tina afterward. Figure 5.2 shows the completed form. It indicates that Miss Tina asked 10 questions during the 20-minute group session. Together they code the questions as *F* for questions requiring facts for answers and *A* for questions requiring students to analyze the facts. Miss Tina points out that the ratio of 6 *F*s to 4 *A*s isn't ideal. But Mrs. Parry tells her that she noticed that most of the factual questions came at the beginning of the session and came really fast because the answers were often quite short; as a result, she could barely write them down. But when Miss Tina asked an *A* question, she had plenty of time in between to listen and write because several students contributed answers. In fact, she had so much time that she started listing the initials of the students who made a contribution. It looked as if Marcie hadn't said anything at all—she had nodded her head and mumbled an agreement once or twice when another student had expressed an opinion, but she really had not given an answer of her own.

Think how useful this single observation was for Miss Tina and Mrs. Parry. Take a moment to list some of the things that you think they learned from the observation, the information that was recorded on the form, and the subsequent discussion.

Miss Tina

_____

_____

_____

_____

_____

_____

_____

_____

Mrs. Parry

_____

_____

_____

_____

_____

_____

_____

_____

Figure 5.2
SAMPLE COMPLETED OBSERVATION FORM

Date: <u>Nov. 1</u>   Time: <u>10:00–10:20 a.m.</u>

Current Area of Focus: Getting students to think about what they read, and specifically the number of questions asked that are high level or low level

---

Observations:	Notes:
Who was the main character in the story? F	A = questions requiring analysis
What year did the story take place? F	F = factual questions
Who was the author? F	
What do you like about this author's work? A (BB, WM, BG, JQ)	
What did Johnny break? F	
Why was this a problem? A (BB, SL, MJM, MB, SW, AM, DA)	
Now they will not be able to go . . . where? F (BB)	
How would you feel if this happened to you? A (JM, DA, BB, KC, JB)	
What did they do to Johnny? F (DA)	
What do you think will happen next? A (BB, JQ, JM, BG, AM, MO)	F = 6 A = 4

Possible Next Area of Focus:
Getting responses from all students—more than once.

Miss Tina gained some very specific information about an aspect of her teaching (asking questions) during that short observation because of the data that Mrs. Parry collected for her. She learned the number and type of questions that she asked, as well as which students responded (and by implication, which did not). Mrs. Parry was provided with a model of a skill that she would subsequently need in her work and an opportunity to focus on the details of that skill through collecting data and discussing it with Miss Tina afterward. She acquired specific information on student understanding and participation in the group discussion, and she also had the opportunity to learn the importance of analyzing one's own classroom practices in order to assess their effectiveness and make changes if necessary.

As you use this procedure with your paraeducator, it is important that you communicate the specifics of what you want observed and recorded. Tell your paraeducator that you are not asking her to judge your performance or speculate about why certain things happened. You just want her to record specific actions, in the same way that Miss Tina asked Mrs. Parry to write down the questions she asked. You may not be altogether comfortable with the idea of being observed by your paraeducator, but we recommend that you use this procedure to enhance her skills and yours so that you both become more aware of the particulars of your everyday classroom practice.

It will take some practice to determine the specific things that you want your paraeducator to watch and record. Here are four steps to follow:

1. Identify what you need (or want) to know about the effectiveness of your teaching.

2. Select a focus for the observation, identifying the specifics of what you want your paraeducator to watch for, that will relate directly to what you want to know about your teaching effectiveness.

3. Decide what data or pieces of information you need so that you can assess the effectiveness of the teaching session, and also decide on the best format for collecting that information (seating chart, tally sheet, etc.).

4. Use the communication skills you have enhanced through what you learned in Chapter 3 to ensure that your paraeducator understands what you want and what she is to write down as she observes.

Figure 5.3 shows a few examples of what other teachers have targeted for observation, what data have been collected, and how the information has been recorded. In addition to these examples, there are many other things you may choose to have your paraeducator observe. In reality, you may be more eager to model good practices for your paraeducator than you are to analyze your own teaching, but this procedure will allow you to do both. Make sure you clearly identify the area you want your paraeducator to observe and the specifics of what she is to record. Teachers find that it is usually not necessary to say, "I want you to observe me doing this because you are so weak in this area." Mature adults learn quickly when their attention is focused and they have an excellent role model.

It may also take practice for the observer to write down only the things that are important to the focus of the observation. It is tempting, especially for teachers, to add an evaluative statement. Much of what we do on any given teaching day is to analyze or judge what needs to happen next. In this case, both you and your paraeducator-observer will need to be careful not to add an evaluation to the data you have recorded. Resist the temptation to write, for example, "Good job!" The person who was observed should make her own interpretation of the facts recorded on the observation form.

As you use this procedure you will find that you get better at identifying the issues you want to address and have observed, and the observer will get better at recording only what she sees and hears, without imposing a judgment. Ideally you should consider conducting observations of each other three or four times a month, so that you create a habit of professional development and start to see results in terms of your confidence and your effectiveness in helping students learn. Then periodically review the aspects of teaching that you have chosen to observe, the progress that you feel you have made, and areas that you feel you still need to work on.

Figure 5.3
EXAMPLES OF OBSERVATION ACTIVITIES

Teacher's Identified Focus of Observation	Data to Be Collected	How Paraeducator Will Record Data
Are all students participating in class discussions?	Number of students answering questions and who they are.	On a seating chart, put a check beside the desk/box of each student who answers a question.
Do as many girls give answers to math problems as boys?	Number of girls and number of boys responding to math problems.	Record tally marks for each person who answers. It may look like this: G = \\\\ B = \\\
Jim is very shy. How often does he volunteer in class?	Number of times Jim raises his hand in class.	Make a note throughout the day of each time Jim raises his hand and volunteers a response.
Am I being as positive as I need to be in class?	Number of times I praise, reward, or encourage a student in an hour.	Choose a 1-hour block and record/count each positive statement I make.
Do I need to be more specific when I praise a student?	What do I say when I reward, encourage, or praise a student?	Identify a specific block of time; write down the things I say to students about their work or behavior.

Summary

Your paraeducator brings many valuable life experiences to the job. Although you may use some of the same teaching techniques to train your paraeducator that you use with your students, recognizing the differences between adult learners and young students is an important consideration. You can supplement your training by directing your paraeducator to the many available resources that she may not be accessing, such as professional organizations and publications.

On-the-job collaboration with another adult allows the teacher and the paraeducator to reflect on their work and its affect on student learning. In a positive and supportive environment, on-the-job training and collaboration provide the best and most relevant kind of professional development. They do not require that one of the instructional team members be away from the classroom for training that may not apply to the actual classroom setting.

It may not be possible for you to provide on-the-job training for your paraeducator in certain areas. For example, medical procedures or other specialized activities may require training and certification from specialized personnel. Your staff development department can most likely help with this kind of training. However, you can provide extensive training to your paraeducator in skills that relate directly to her classroom responsibilities by using the observation procedure described in this chapter. Referring your paraeducator to magazines, paraprofessional training conferences, and newsletters will also provide training and support. Being an advocate for training for your paraeducator in these ways will help her to strengthen the instructional team, and everyone will benefit.

In Practice

The following are some suggestions for ways in which you can apply what you have learned in this chapter to your own work situation. We also have provided space for you to add ideas that you glean from your own experience and interactions with colleagues.

• Avoid the temptation to just give your paraeducator your college textbooks to read in order to provide her with information needed for her work. She may not have attended college, or it may be a long time since she was a student, and reading from the textbook may just be too daunting. If the book has passages or a few pages that are useful, with information presented in a way that will help her to see the application to her work, you might mark them and ask her to read them. But make clear that she does not have to read the whole text and that you will talk to her about what she has read soon afterward so that you can discuss how she can apply the information to her work. Remember, too, that few paraeducators are paid to do homework.

• Be aware of how you speak to other people. Matching their tone of voice, rate of speech, and choice of vocabulary helps to build rapport and to make others feel that they count and are respected. This is an important first step in providing training for your paraeducator because it shows that you wish to communicate effectively with her.

• Value the life experiences your paraeducator brings to the classroom. For example, a paraeducator who is bilingual can deeply enrich the instructional team as well as relate to students who are also bilingual. Valuing her in this way also shows her that you recognize and appreciate her skills, abilities, and viewpoints, and that these are things the two of you can build upon.

• People should not be expected to perform tasks that they have not been taught or that have not been modeled for them. Provide learning support for your paraeducator by ensuring that she has the opportunity to learn before she is expected to perform. Model the task for her and discuss it before asking her to demonstrate her own skill.

• _____

_____

_____

• _____

_____

_____

- _____
_____
_____

Setting Priorities for Improvement

Now that you have read the chapter on providing on-the-job training for your paraeducator and have had an opportunity to consider how this applies to your work situation, take some time to set priorities for your work in this area. Choose one aspect of providing on-the-job training, list one or two ways in which you think you can improve in this area, decide how you will know if you have made improvements, determine ways in which you might keep a record and use it to chart improvement, and then set a date when you will review these priorities and adjust your plans if necessary.

I would like to improve in the following aspect of providing on-the-job training:

_____

_____

I will take the following actions to bring about change:

_____

_____

_____

_____

_____

I will measure improvement or success in the following ways:

_____

_____

_____

_____

I will keep a record of what I do and changes I may see by doing the following:

_____

_____

_____

_____

I will review progress toward this priority on this date: _____

Creating a
Feedback Loop

6

We have already discussed the importance of establishing open and effective communication channels with your paraeducator. In this chapter we deal with a specific aspect of communication relating to the on-the-job training procedure described in Chapter 5, in which we discussed how you can use observation to provide a model of effective teaching and classroom management for your paraeducator. We help you use the information gained from the observation to develop feedback that will support staff development for your paraeducator. These are the questions we address:

- How can you create a feedback loop to ensure that your paraeducator is aware of what she is learning?
- How can you provide nonjudgmental feedback for your paraeducator?

Creating a Feedback Loop

How can you create a feedback loop to ensure that your paraeducator is aware of what she is learning? The usefulness of what you do to train your paraeducator—such as the observation and data collection procedure that we outlined in Chapter 5—will be very limited if you do not establish some mechanism for providing feedback on what you and she have observed and collected data on. This may seem a somewhat obvious statement, but the point cannot be overemphasized: the discussions that you have about your work are every bit as important as the observations and various data collection or recording procedures that you use. Those data collection and recording procedures provide a focus for your discussions and concrete evidence of your instructional practices and effectiveness, but without the discussion they may be fairly meaningless. Your paraeducator needs you to help interpret and provide a context for the information she gathers and the things she sees. You need her to provide another perspective on your work so that you can both improve.

Compare this feedback loop for your paraeducator with the feedback that you give your students. Why do you give them feedback? The most important reason is to help them to be aware of what they are learning and to firmly establish that learning in their minds. The feedback that you give them helps them to know if they are "right," and if they have understood correctly. It also increases their confidence in their own skills and abilities, so that they know that they have a firm foundation to build on. These same good reasons apply to giving your paraeducator feedback: you establish for her some of the "right" (most effective) ways of providing instruction to students and managing the classroom environment; you help her learn the vocabulary of educational terms for the teaching techniques she can use and discuss with others; you help her to become aware of her increasing skills; and you assist her in building confidence in her ability to work effectively and make further improvements.

Feedback is most helpful when it is specific. Detailed feedback is considered *formative*—that is, it informs people about what they have done and therefore produces learning and enables them to make changes if necessary. On the other hand, telling someone "You did a good job on this" is an example of *summative* feedback—it sums up what the person has done but does not explain what was good or bad about it. The grades that you assign students at the end of the semester or year are summative feedback. But if you want to know exactly what a student has learned, and what you can therefore teach them next, you need formative feedback—test scores, examples of their work, and other details. Likewise, you need to provide detail in the feedback that you give your students and your paraeducator so that they know where they stand, what they have done well, and where they need to improve.

A specific example can clarify these concepts. Let's take our example from Chapter 5, with Mrs. Parry observing Miss Tina. You will recall that they wanted to determine the number of high-level and low-level questions that they were asking their students to respond to. They felt that asking more high-level questions—those requiring analysis—would cause the students to think more about what they were reading. Referring to the sample observation form that Mrs. Parry and Miss Tina used (Figure 5.2), we asked you to write what you thought each of them learned from the information they collected during the observation. We said that looking at observational data and setting goals for improvement based on that data would help your instructional team build confidence and effectiveness in helping students learn. However, if you are to gain the most from this activity, you must make it a formal process.

An action worksheet such as that provided in Figure 6.1 will help you determine what actions you and your paraeducator should take as a result of the observation. It formalizes the feedback loop so that each of you knows what to expect from the other. After an observation, complete the action worksheet together. Write a brief description of what you focused on for this observation. (In the case of Mrs. Parry and Miss Tina, it would be "The number of high-level and low-level questions.") Now write what the two of you learned from the information you recorded. The things you learned from your teacher perspective and the things your paraeducator learned from her perspective may be similar or different, but make sure you record them all. Now together think of the actions you will take as a result of the information you gathered. For example, if you, like Mrs. Parry and Miss Tina, were focusing on questions asked during reading group discussions, some of the actions your paraeducator could take would be "Recognize students who are responding" and "Work to get those who are not responding to participate." Actions you as the teacher could take would be "Provide support by coteaching the group discussion" or "Provide examples of high-level and low-level questions related to the reading material." Write these actions down, being sure to state who is to take the action—you or your paraeducator or both. Beware of listing too many actions; prioritize and focus first on those that you feel will be most helpful.

Completing the action worksheet helps to complete the feedback loop. You have focused on an area for improvement, observed it in the context of student

Figure 6.1
OBSERVATION ACTION WORKSHEET

This action worksheet will help you to become more aware of the learning process that will occur as you observe and are observed teaching. It will also help you to move forward and take action based on what you are learning.

Focus of the Observation	What I Learned from the Data	Action I Will Take as a Result of What I Learned

learning, and then analyzed it together and brainstormed new actions to take as a result of what you have discussed and learned. As you finish this last step, you have communicated and perhaps clarified the expectations of each team member about the actions that will be taken. Include the action worksheet in a three-ring binder with the observation forms. Periodically review the aspects of teaching and classroom management that you have chosen to observe, the progress that you feel you have made, and the areas that you feel you still need to work on. You will likely feel a great sense of accomplishment as you see how far your team has come in its own staff development efforts.

Of course, you can provide feedback for your paraeducator in several other ways. You will need to be sensitive to her preferences, as well as your own, as you decide on the best method of doing this. Here are some suggestions for making the feedback effective, whichever method you choose:

• Set a time each week when you will meet to discuss your work. This should not be a time when you also handle scheduling and organizational arrangements, relegating the feedback portion to whatever time is left at the end; scheduling and organization should be part of a different discussion.

• Avoid an open-ended format for the discussion. Although it is sometimes useful to ask, "So, do you have any questions about our work?" this approach is not likely to be effective in helping you to focus on a particular topic. Your para-educator may be reluctant to launch into a discussion of a controversial topic; if her concerns relate to aspects of classroom management, she may not want to appear critical of what you do; or she may simply not know enough about what needs to be discussed. Choose a topic that is common to both of your roles, be prepared to share your ideas and concerns about your own work, and then ask her what she thinks about the topic or if she has any concerns about this aspect of her own work. If she is more concerned about other things, they may well emerge from the discussion.

• Choose an aspect of your work to focus on for the whole semester. Establishing a focus at the beginning of the semester and from the start of your discussions indicates the importance that you assign to that aspect of your work and communicates the idea that even apparently insignificant components of the instructional process may need fairly extensive attention and improvements.

Providing Nonjudgmental Feedback

How can you provide nonjudgmental feedback for your paraeducator? In our earlier discussion about monitoring the quality of your paraeducator's work, we emphasized that it is important to make clear that observation and monitoring of what other adults do in the classroom is an acceptable activity. We suggested ways in which you can encourage your paraeducator to watch what you do, as a means of learning the skills required of her in her role. Similarly, you need to clearly tell your paraeducator that giving feedback is part of that monitoring process. Of course, feedback comes in many forms, as discussed in Chapter 3, "Improving Communications," and feedback can be negative or positive, critical or constructive. We recommend that you establish a habit of using only a positive, nonjudgmental mode of feedback.

In one sense, all feedback is judgmental, and even if you do not "pass judgment" on your paraeducator's work, she will probably know whether you approve or disapprove of what she is doing. However, feedback may be considered nonjudgmental if it conforms to these two criteria:

• The feedback focuses on the actions, not on the person; the paraeducator should have no sense of personal criticism.

• The feedback is based on facts that directly relate to the paraeducator's work, not on opinions, personality, or personal attributes.

When you provide feedback to your paraeducator on her work, she needs to know whether what she is doing is effective. Specific feedback designed to increase effectiveness is much more likely to be motivating than personal compliments, and it will certainly be more instructive and indicative of your support for her and her work. You should, however, be sensitive to the fact that even when you state the facts, your paraeducator may feel that she is inadequate or not doing as well as she should. Remember that you need to help her become accustomed to receiving feedback. When you first establish this procedure of giving frequent and detailed feedback, you may need to keep reassuring her that you are doing it to build on the skills she already possesses and that it is a process that you engage in also as a teacher. It may take time for both of you to become comfortable with this process.

Summary

It is important to complete the cycle of monitoring your paraeducator's work and providing on-the-job training by providing feedback. This instructs her and helps her to become more aware of her own learning. Providing feedback to your paraeducator is much like providing feedback to your students, which also helps them to take more responsibility for their own learning. Providing feedback is another way in which you provide a role model for your paraeducator: you model not only effective instruction, but also professionalism, as you engage in a process of ongoing self-evaluation and take responsibility for your own professional development.

In Practice

Following are some suggestions for ways in which you can apply what you have learned in this chapter to your own working situation. We also have allowed space for you to add ideas that you glean from your own experience and interactions with colleagues.

• Make a list of the things that you generally say to your paraeducator when you want to show approval of what she has done. For each one, ask yourself, Does this statement teach my paraeducator anything about effective practice? Have I helped her to understand what was good about what she did? Was my comment specific enough to help her know exactly what she should do the next time this situation arises? If the answer to any of these questions is no, you may wish to add to your list some different things that you could say to her when she does something that is effective. Making comments such as "Good job!" suggests that you have evaluated your paraeducator's work as being good or bad. More specific, nonjudgmental statements would be "Bobbi raised his hand five times during that 10-minute session—once each time you asked a question" or "Jodi was out of her seat three times, but each time she returned to her chair, you said, 'Thank you for sitting down, Jodi.'"

• Provide a mini-training session before your paraeducator observes you to ensure that she understands the meaning of nonjudgmental statements and the need to make only factual comments. Help her to understand that you have no objection to positive statements, compliments, or praise, but that it is much more informative and helpful to you when you're trying to make improvements if she merely states the facts.

• _____

_____

_____

• _____

_____

_____

• _____

_____

_____

Setting Priorities for Improvement

Now that you have read the chapter on creating a feedback loop for your paraeducator and have had an opportunity to consider how this applies to the situation you work in, we suggest that you take some time to set priorities for your work in this area. Choose an aspect of creating a feedback loop, list one or two ways in which you think you can improve in this area, decide how you will know if you have made improvements, determine ways in which you might keep a record and use it to chart improvement, then set a date when you will review these priorities and adjust your plans if necessary.

I would like to improve in the following aspect of creating a feedback loop:

_____

_____

I will take the following actions to bring about change:

_____

_____

_____

_____

_____

_____

I will measure improvement or success in the following ways:

_____

_____

_____

_____

I will keep a record of what I do and changes I may see by doing the following:

_____

_____

_____

_____

I will review progress toward this priority on this date: _____

The Logistics

7

An issue that teachers frequently raise when they want to improve their supervisory skills and teamwork with their paraeducators is time: time to observe, time to plan together, time to discuss observations. They want to know how to find time in an already busy schedule, given the many demands made on teachers and paraeducators, and how to persuade school or school district administrators to provide that time. The questions we address in this chapter are these:

- How can you find the time to work with and train your paraeducator?
- How can you enlist the support of your administrators?

Finding Time

How can you find the time to work with and train your paraeducator? The most frequent response we get when we ask classroom teams "Where did you find the time?" is this: "We just made the time to do it." When we probe, we discover that it was not always that simple, and, in fact, they found many creative ways to "just make time" to work together by observing each other and planning their work. We list some of those ways below. We take their response as an indication of the priority that they are willing to give to observation and to the professional dialogue that can arise from it, and we applaud them for continuing to strive for improvement. Here are some of their suggestions:

- Good communication is a vital element of classroom efficiency. Talk to each other whenever you can; send notes if you have to, but make sure that everyone knows what they need to know so that work is not duplicated and so that no one is frustrated by being left in the dark about procedures or expectations.

• Plan on conducting your observations when you have another adult in the classroom in addition to yourself and your paraeducator, such as a parent volunteer or a student teacher. Although it is important that you supervise their work also, you can take one session per week when they are in the classroom and divide the class in such a way that you and your paraeducator have a group to work with and observe while the parent or student teacher works with the remainder.

• If you wish to work with just a small group and you feel that it is inappropriate to ask the parent or student teacher to work with more than a few students, organize group work and assignments that the students can work on independently or cooperatively. If you regularly schedule group work sessions, you not only will have multiple opportunities to conduct observations and discuss your work with your paraeducator, but you also will increase your students' ability to work cooperatively and on their own.

• If your paraeducator has no preparation time scheduled, use some of the time you control to give her this time in your classroom. Do not schedule her to work directly with students for all the time she is with you. Think of how much time you spend preparing for teaching and consider it a wise investment to make this gift of time to your paraeducator.

• If you work with more than one paraeducator, your supervisory responsibilities increase, of course; but you also have more possibilities for providing support and mentoring if you train them to observe each other. Once they become used to the procedure, they can observe and take data independently and even discuss what they have found. You can then discuss the observation with the one paraeducator who was observed, or with both of them. Decisions about what can be done to improve practice will always require your input and approval, but as they become more proficient at the process, you will not need to be directly involved in every aspect of it.

• Involve students in the data collection and observation process. You should choose your area of focus carefully if you involve students, but a valuable dimension is added to the process when they become more aware of their own behavior and learning. For example, if you have each student tally the number of times he or she responds to a question during a discussion or the number of times the person teaching asks them a question, you make the students more aware of their own level of participation, and you also gain data that tell you and your paraeducator about the effectiveness of your classroom practices.

• Although the ultimate purpose of conducting observations and increasing the effectiveness of your teamwork is to help students learn more easily, focus on collecting data on your own practice rather than on the behavior or reactions of the students. As you learn to use more effective instructional and behavior management practices, your students will inevitably benefit. Focusing on your practice simplifies the procedure because you have to collect data at only one level (the teacher level rather than both the teacher and learner levels). Besides, you cannot change student behavior without changing your own. You have control over your own behavior, so start there and the student responses will improve.

• When you and your paraeducator find yourselves with a spare 5 or 10 minutes—even if it's between classes or when you're waiting in the lunch line—use them to discuss observations and effective practices, rather than just wasting them on social chit-chat. (Do be aware of confidentiality if the conversation can be overheard.) You'll set a good example for other faculty, staff, and students when they hear you engaging in professional dialogue as often as possible.

• Assign routine, minor responsibilities to students. Such things as roll call, distribution of papers, and other small tasks can take up a great deal of one person's time, but if they are shared among several students they will take each person only a few minutes to complete. In this way you can help students learn to take responsibility for aspects of classroom organization, save the few minutes you or your paraeducator might spend on performing all of those tasks yourselves, and use them more productively for your own professional development.

• Get into the habit of writing a brief outline of things you want to discuss when you next meet with your paraeducator. If you write them down, you have a chance to think about what is most important so that you do not waste valuable time covering minor points. And if you give your paraeducator the outline before you meet, she can add items that she would like to discuss. It also gives her an opportunity to think about the items beforehand so that she doesn't have to make on-the-spot decisions, and it allows her to gather information she may need for the meeting.

• Whenever possible, communicate in writing for small matters that really do not require a meeting. Use a log or notebook, post-its, or even e-mail. This is especially useful if your paraeducator's working day starts as the students come into the classroom or if she comes into your room later in the day. You can leave notes or reminders of things that you would like her to do without having to disrupt the flow of your teaching by stopping to give instructions when she arrives in the room. Likewise, if she leaves the classroom before the end of the day, she can leave you notes about what she has done with the students she has been working with and any concerns she may have. We would not recommend that you communicate only in this way, but it can be an efficient way to cover simple items without disrupting the class.

• Some teachers use the time while they are driving to work to call their paraeducator on a cell phone. Of course, you should be careful while driving; but if you are stuck in traffic, this can be a useful way to spend even 10 minutes catching up with each other and making last-minute adjustments to your plans for the day. Likewise at the end of the day, if it is convenient for both of you, you can do some useful debriefing on the phone as you drive home.

Enlisting the Support of Administrators

How can you enlist the support of your administrators? You may be fortunate enough to work under an administrator who includes some preparation time in your paraeducator's schedule. If not, you might want to petition for it, on the grounds that she needs time to prepare (particularly if she spends a large portion of her time instructing students) in order to be effective. The investment of just 30 minutes per week is well worth the potential positive effects, although more preparation time would be even better. You can point out to your administrator that this time allocation is crucial if you are expected to provide training for your paraeducator in all of her classroom responsibilities, particularly those relating to instruction, which requires substantial training in a wide range of skills.

No doubt your administrator provides support for you and your paraeducator in many ways. Take a moment to think about and write down the things that your school or district administration already does to support your classroom instructional team.

- _____
- _____
- _____
- _____
- _____

You may have listed such things as inviting paraeducators to faculty meetings and school-based inservice training, providing a differentiated pay scale according to years of classroom experience, or subscribing to education resources and making them available to school staff. Administrators may not often receive acknowledgment or recognition for the efforts they make, but if you do take the time to show appreciation, you are, of course, more likely to encourage continuation of the supportive practices. You might consider providing your administrator with feedback on a training opportunity or use of release time. A brief paragraph about what you learned lets the administrator know that you gained something from the experience. Be sure to give formative feedback based on facts relevant to your work and that of your paraeducator. It would also be useful for you to outline the observation procedure that you are using with your paraeducator to let your administrator know that you are providing on-the-job training directly relevant to your paraeducator's roles. You might also suggest the use of a similar procedure if a formal, annual evaluation is to be carried out for your paraeducator.

Summary

You may need to be very creative in order to find the time to collaborate with your paraeducator, particularly if she works in your classroom for only part of the day. The effort is definitely worthwhile, however, and suggestions from other educators should help you to begin that process. In addition, look for ways in which you can enlist the help of your school or district administrators in this process—and be sure to acknowledge their support.

In Practice

Almost all of this chapter could fall under the "In Practice" heading, because it focuses on the various practical ways in which you can organize for more effective supervision. This section provides some additional ideas for organizing your supervisory work. We also have provided space for you to add ideas you may glean from your own experience or from interactions with colleagues.

• Keep a "consultation log" in an easily accessible place; you and your paraeducator can record brief notes in it so that the next person knows what to do to pick up where the last person left off a task.

• Prepare an agenda for your teacher-paraeducator meetings and stick to it! Don't talk about personal matters until you've gone through everything on the agenda. Instructional teams that do this find that they accomplish more toward the goal of helping students but still have fun in the process.

• E-mail is a great tool. If you have a computer in your classroom, you and your paraeducator can type notes to each other. Even if you work in the classroom together, this can be a good way of keeping track of what is happening and passing information along.

• A teacher we know developed templates on her computer for notes to parents, to other teachers, and to the administration. Because much of the information was already written in, in most cases she simply had to write a few sentences for each new letter.

• A resource teacher we visited carried a pager that was set on the vibrating signal rather than a buzzer. She was assigned to supervise many paraeducators who worked in various classrooms. The paraeducators could page her when she was urgently needed.

• If you have a paraeducator who is assigned to other teachers in addition to you, consider how you can be an advocate for her and in what ways you can facilitate the communication process. Conversing with the other teachers can help you reduce the stress of a paraeducator who works for multiple teachers (bosses) and has heavy and varied workloads without much decision-making authority. Poor coordination among teachers can add to this stress, but you can take steps to reduce it by checking schedules and expectations.

• _____

_____

_____

• _____

_____

_____

• _____

_____

_____

Setting Priorities for Improvement

Now that you have read about logistics and organization and have had an opportunity to consider how this applies to the situation you work in, take some time to set priorities for your work in this area. Choose an aspect of logistics and organization, list one or two ways in which you think you can improve in this area, decide how you will know if you have made improvements, determine ways in which you might keep a record and use it to chart improvement, and then set a date when you will review these priorities and adjust your plans if necessary.

I would like to improve in the following aspect of logistics and organization:

_____

_____

I will take the following actions to bring about change:

_____

_____

_____

_____

_____

I will measure improvement or success in the following ways:

_____

_____

_____

_____

I will keep a record of what I do and changes I may see by doing the following:

_____

_____

_____

_____

I will review progress toward this priority on this date: _____

Troubleshooting 8

In this chapter we give you some suggestions for what we hope will be the rare occasions when you encounter roadblocks in the successful supervision of your paraeducator. We cover what we have found to be some of the most common difficulties encountered by teachers, as well as the solutions that they have suggested, and discuss them as a series of "what if" questions. The two major questions we address are these:

- What if your paraeducator resists your offers of providing training for her and becomes defensive when you offer her resources and information?
- What if, despite the training you provide in the classroom or training that your paraeducator receives through the school district, her skills in certain areas do not improve?

If you find yourself in one of the situations outlined in this chapter, you should first examine what you have done (or not done). Reviewing each of the suggested chapters will be helpful. However, sometimes you reach a point at which you can do no more. When you work with other people, you have to accept that they may see things very differently from you. Even if they agree with you in principle, they may not be quite as eager as you are to put the principles into practice. Don't forget: you are probably not just an average teacher. The fact that you are reading this book and trying to enhance your skills and make improvements to your classroom suggests that you are constantly striving for higher standards in your work and want to do everything possible to make that happen. Not everyone is that committed.

Dealing with Resistance

What if your paraeducator resists your offers of providing training and becomes defensive when you offer her resources and information? Several reasons may account for your paraeducator's resistance. Consider some of the following:

- *Your paraeducator's age and classroom experience.* If she is older than you or has more classroom experience than you do, she may resent being told what to do by a "youngster." Be smart: benefit from her age and experience and ask her advice on classroom and teaching matters. Although you, the teacher, are responsible for providing effective instruction to your students and therefore should not support ineffective or harmful practices, it will be more helpful over the long term for you to initially concede some preferences than to insist on having your own way. This will show that you have confidence in your paraeducator and wish to work collaboratively and harmoniously with her. She may know the students better than you do and be able to offer wise advice. Look back to Chapter 1, where we suggested that you consider your paraeducator's skills and experience, and then look at Chapter 3, where you decided how you could use her strengths and preferences to help you function more effectively as a team. Consider what you wrote there and think of ways in which you can draw on that experience for the benefit of the students. Start there, with something that you know your paraeducator is good at and is willing to help with, and it should be much easier to add other things or make modifications later.

- *Your paraeducator's prior educational experiences.* It may be many years since your paraeducator completed formal schooling; she may have completed only high school and have no college experience; she may see herself as someone who does not learn easily and may associate training with studying, extensive reading, tests, and written assignments. Think about the format of the training that you have been offering. You may well have taken the same sort of approach that you experienced in college or that you now experience when you go to inservice training. Consider whether there might be a better way to approach the training. Perhaps just calling it "training" is intimidating for her. Much of what you are going to do with her is to have her think about what she does and brainstorm ways in which it can be done better. So perhaps you can use less intimidating vocabulary by being descriptive and specific. For example, "Let's see how our use of high-level and low-level questions can help students to think about what they read" is much more informative and direct than "I'm not sure that students are cognitively engaged in their reading material."

Dealing with Lack of Improvement

What if, despite the training you provide in the classroom or training your paraeducator receives through the school district, her skills in certain areas do not improve? Just as you add to the difficulty of the assignments you give students according to how well they have mastered the necessary skills, so too you should assign your paraeducator only tasks for which she is qualified and competent. As her skills improve, you can ask her to accept more complex assignments. As the classroom professional, you have a responsibility to ensure that your paraeducator actually adds something to the educational process. However, you must recognize that she—like you—has both strengths and weaknesses, and as a team you can compensate for each other. Consider the following points:

• If the paraeducator is not making as much of a contribution as you would like in a particular area of instruction, ask yourself if she is nevertheless making some contribution. For example, she may not be skilled in using positive methods to deal with disruptive behavior, but she may have good relationships with the students and be able to communicate well with them. You have two choices. If the disadvantages outweigh the advantages and you feel that she is not making any positive contribution in the classroom role you are concerned about, then it is better not to have her work in that role at all. But if you feel that her contribution is useful, then persist and find ways to use the skills she already has to teach her the additional skills she needs. Talk to her—in this case about how well she manages to develop relationships with the students, the skills that help her to do that, and how you would like her to adapt those skills to handling disruptions in a positive way. Note that this use of a positive approach models a skill you want her to acquire for working with students.

  • Consider whether it would be more appropriate, and make better use of her skills, if she worked one-on-one with a student rather than with a group. For example, if she finds it difficult to organize for or give attention to several students at once but is good at instructing individual students, then have her work with one student at a time. Similarly, if her behavior management skills are not sufficient to control disruptions in a group of students but she has good instructional skills, she can still make a contribution by teaching one student at a time. It is far better to have her work well with individual students than to have disruptions and ineffective practice by insisting that she work with a group.

You are the leader of your classroom instructional team, and you can be as creative as you wish in deciding how best to use your paraeducator's skills and strengths. There are no standard roles for paraeducators and no standard procedures for effective supervision. You'll need to adapt the suggestions in this book to fit your situation and working style as well as your paraeducator's style and skills. Effective supervision is a matter of working on the positive attributes your paraeducator brings to her work and putting them to best use.

Practicing What You've Learned

9

Chapters 1 through 7 include an "In Practice" section with suggestions to help you translate the information from the chapter into your classroom practice. This chapter provides you with opportunities to apply your knowledge to two case studies that relate to the supervision of paraeducators. In each case you are given some information and asked to react to it given what you now know about effective supervision of paraeducators. The information is in the form of a description—by a paraeducator—of some of her daily activities and responsibilities. After your response, we guide you through some areas of additional consideration.

Case Study 1: Mrs. Nielson

Your paraeducator, Mrs. Nielson, is a young woman who has been working part-time in your classroom for the past semester. You feel that you have made a good start on working together. She has good interpersonal skills and is eager to do her job well and learn new skills. On the first day of the new semester, she comes into your class as usual in the afternoon, and as soon as she has an opportunity, she relates the following:

> Do you remember that I told you I'd been assigned to work in the new history teacher's class? Well, I went into the teachers lounge this morning to see if I could meet him and check what he wanted me to do today. Everyone was visiting or doing last-minute things, so I just hung around a bit hoping that someone would notice I was there; but no one said anything, so I just sort of called out, "Is there a Mr. Brown here?" A young man got up and came toward me, introduced himself, and shook my hand. He seemed very friendly. So I told him my name and

that I was his new paraeducator and was just wondering what he wanted me to do.

He gave me directions to his classroom and said, "I have a couple of things to do in the office"; so I thought he'd just want me to go down to the room and wait for him, perhaps make myself useful, you know. But then as he was heading off toward the office he said, "So if you can go and get the class started, I'll be along in 10 minutes." Can you imagine? I was so surprised I couldn't even speak! And then he'd left, so I had no choice but to go and see to the class.

I was just terrified—it was a 10th grade class—I had no idea what he was going to start working on or what they'd been doing last semester. And I didn't know what they'd be like with me—you know, with my only being a paraeducator I thought perhaps they wouldn't listen to me or settle down. As it happened, I went in there and it was OK. They asked me if I was the new teacher, and when I said no, I was a paraeducator and Mr. Brown would be along shortly, they wanted to know what a paraeducator was—you know the district has changed our title so the kids still call us "aides." So I told them, and they wanted to know how I got to be a paraeducator and did you have to go to college and get training, those sorts of things. They seemed really interested, so when Mr. Brown turned up we were still talking about it, and everything was OK. But I don't think I could do that very often. What do you think I should do about it?

1. What steps would you advise Mrs. Nielson to take in order to clarify Mr. Brown's expectations of her?

_____

_____

_____

_____

_____

2. Why is it appropriate for a paraeducator to ask a teacher for clarification of responsibilities and expectations?

_____

_____

_____

_____

_____

3. What might Mrs. Nielson's story prompt you to do in order to enhance the working relationship you have with her and to help her to be more effective?

_____

_____

_____

_____

_____

4. If you had overall responsibility for paraeducators in the school, what support or information could you offer to Mr. Brown and other teachers like him who work with paraeducators in their classrooms? How would you provide this support and information?

_____

_____

_____

_____

_____

As you wrote your answers, you may have looked back through Chapter 1, reviewed the responsibilities of the leader of the classroom instructional team, and reflected on the things you found you could work on with your paraeducator to enhance instruction. As you review your responses to Questions 1 and 2 of the case study, do not forget to assess whether your answers meet the legal responsibilities of your job description as well as that of your paraeducator. You may also have used information from Chapters 2 and 3 and considered the ways in which you can clarify and communicate roles and responsibilities. Your answer to Question 4 should include the principles of effective instruction, which apply to adult learners, both paraprofessional and professional, as well as to students.

Case Study 2: Mrs. Davis

I'm Mrs. Davis, and my job responsibility is student evaluation. I work at a middle school, and my direct supervisor is the special education teacher. But I don't work in the resource room; I spend a lot of time giving tests to students, so I have a little room to myself that's partly for paper storage with a table and two chairs. I take my students there so that there are no distractions for them when they're being tested. These are all students with IEPs, but a lot of them are included in regular classes for at least part of the day—usually the first part, because they seem to be able to settle in better in the regular classes in the morning, and then they spend most afternoons in the resource room. But as I say, I don't spend much time in there because I do all of the testing and keep the files up to date, and that takes up all of my time. It helps the resource teacher a lot because it's so time consuming, and, really, her skills can be better used trying to teach the students rather than just doing endless paperwork.

So what I do is check the student files at the beginning of the week to see who's due for a three-year evaluation, and I make myself a list of who I'm going to see each day. I leave a copy of the list for the resource teacher so that she knows who I'm testing that week, and sometimes she has students who need extra tests so she'll give me a list; but usually I just work my way through the files. It takes the best part of the morning to do all of the testing for each student, because I also have to interpret the results and record them. And, of course, I only work part-time anyway, and my lunchroom supervision takes up the rest of my day. So in the morning, I see who's on my list, and I go and collect them from which-ever classroom they're in and they stay with me for most of the rest of the morning. If we finish a little early, I usually keep them with me, because it would be in the middle of the last hour before lunch, and I don't like to disturb the teachers by sending them back then.

The other thing I do is send out notices of upcoming IEP meetings. That's to let parents know when the meeting will be held and to make sure they can come. I also notify the classroom teachers, the special education teacher, and the assistant principal—and the school psy-chologist and speech therapist if they need to come to the meeting. Of course, I have to get the date and time from the assistant principal, but then I send out the notices and make sure all of the paperwork is ready and copied. I've made up my own "Notice of Meeting" form to give the subject teachers—the ones whose classes the students are included in during the mornings—so that they know that they can come to the IEP meetings as well. I also substitute for the resource teacher if she has IEP meetings—usually just for a few hours or a day, but I have sometimes done it for a whole week.

I enjoy my job. I've worked in this school since it opened 15 years ago. My two youngest children came here, and I know a lot of the stu-dents and their parents because I live in the neighborhood. I used to work just a couple of hours a day—supervising recess, duplicating papers, things like that—but when the chance came up to increase my hours and work in the resource room, I thought, why not? That was under the previous resource teacher, and organization just wasn't her thing, so I offered to help with the files. She handed them over to me to organize, and it just evolved from there really—they became my responsibility and the testing sort of came with it.

In light of what you know about effective supervisory practices, consider the following questions. If you were the resource teacher in this situation,

1. What steps might you want to take to increase the level of communication between yourself and Mrs. Davis?

_____

_____

_____

_____

_____

_____

2. What about confidentiality? How does this relate to Mrs. Davis's role of evaluator and record keeper and the limits you might want to set on that role?

_____

_____

_____

_____

_____

_____

3. What other steps would you take to supervise Mrs. Davis's work?

_____

_____

_____

_____

_____

If you were a subject teacher and some students with IEPs attend your class,

1. What would you do to improve communication between you and Mrs. Davis? Is there anyone else you might want to improve communications with?

_____

_____

_____

_____

_____

2. In what ways might you be considered Mrs. Davis's supervisor? What supervisory responsibilities do you think you might have for Mrs. Davis?

_____

_____

_____

_____

_____

3. What role do you think you should play in the IEP process as part of the instructional team?

_____

_____

_____

_____

After you have written your responses to each of the questions regarding Mrs. Davis, look back through Chapter 1 and review your responsibilities as leader of the classroom instructional team. Reflect on the ways you found that you could work with Mrs. Davis in relation to the issues discussed in the chapter. Assess your responses to see if they meet legal requirements of your school district or state. Your answer to Question 2 may include the integration of your supervisory responsibilities into the daily routine of the classroom. It may also include specific training on legal issues offered by the staff development office or the special education department. Question 3 relates to Chapters 1 and 2 again as you clarify roles and responsibilities and then use the skills discussed in Chapter 3—"Improving Communications."

Providing a Safety Net

In each of these case studies, things seem to be going well enough for the moment, even though the cases raise some issues in terms of roles, responsibilities, and more serious legal issues. As they say, however, an ounce of prevention is worth a pound of cure. To begin with, it is important to ensure that your paraeducator (or the paraeducator in the case study) is working within the legal requirements of the job. Training within the classroom or from outside—from the staff development department, for example—can provide the necessary safeguards for such things as the limits of a paraeducator's role, confidentiality, and professional behavior guidelines. You provide a safety net for your paraeducator when you deter preventable problems by taking action as soon as you become aware of the situation. Both of these case studies are based upon actual paraeducator job descriptions and experiences, and they offer helpful reminders of ways in which you can provide effective supervision to the paraeducator who works in your classroom.

Challenge and Reward

Supervision of paraeducators can be a challenge for new teachers and veterans alike, and that challenge may be renewed each time you are assigned to work with a different paraeducator. However, supervision of paraeducators can also be a very rewarding role. It offers you, as the leader of the classroom instructional team, many benefits: another adult perspective in the classroom, someone else's lifetime of experiences and skills, another pair of hands and eyes to help you learn more about your own effectiveness as an educator; an opportunity to facilitate another adult's learning and professional development; and (in the experience of most teacher-paraeducator teams that we have encountered) a tremendous source of support for the important work you do as an educator.

The information and suggestions in this book were generated by our teaching experience and through our work with teachers and paraeducators. They should serve you well as you seek to master your role as supervisor of paraeducators and classroom executive.

References and Resources

References

Beebe, S. A., Beebe, S. J., & Redmond, M. V. (1999). *Interpersonal communication: Relating to others*. Boston, MA: Allyn & Bacon.

Berliner, D. (1989). The nature of expertise in teaching. In F. K. Oser, A. Dick, & J. L. Patry (Eds.), *Effective and responsible teaching* (pp. 227–248). San Francisco: Jossey-Bass.

Hofmeister, A. M. (1991). *Paraprofessionals in special education: Alternatives to casteism*. Paper presented for the Mountain Plains Regional Resource Center Advisory Committee Meeting, Kansas City, MO.

Learn, R. L. (1988, June). *Supervision of paraprofessional workers in special needs vocational education*. Paper presented at the Pennsylvania Vocational Education Conference, Champion, PA.

Pickett, A. L. (1997). Paraeducators in school settings: Framing the issues. In A. L. Pickett & K. Gerlach (Eds.), *Supervising paraeducators in school settings: A team approach*. Austin, TX: Pro-Ed.

Sergiovanni, T. J., & Starratt, R. J. (1993). *Supervision: A redefinition*. New York: McGraw-Hill.

Resources

The following is a brief list of organizations that can provide useful information for paraeducators and teachers.

Association for Supervision and Curriculum Development (ASCD). ASCD is an international association dedicated to teaching and learning for the success of all learners. ASCD offers memberships, books, newsletters, a magazine, a journal, videos, audios, conferences, workshops, and online courses. Web address: http://www.ascd.org

American Federation of Teachers (AFT). The AFT offers membership and a variety of resources to both teachers and paraeducators. It sponsors an annual Paraprofessionals and School-Related Personnel (PSRP) conference. Web address: http://www.aft.org

Council for Exceptional Children (CEC). The CEC is a national special education organization that has made special efforts recently to recruit paraeducators. One of the CEC publications, "Teaching Exceptional Children," includes a "Paraeducator Supervision Notebook" column. Web address: http://www.cec.sped.org

National Education Association (NEA). The NEA has local affiliates in most states. Membership in the national organization is available to paraeducators and other education support personnel (ESP). Web address: http://www.nea.org

National Resource Center for Paraprofessionals in Education and Related Services (NRCP). The NRCP is a national organization that provides training materials and technical assistance, as well as an annual conference and a newsletter, *New Directions*. Web address: http://www.nrcpara.org

National Staff Development Council (NSDC). The NSDC is a large national organization dedicated to providing extensive staff development opportunities to educators through conferences and publications. Web address: http://www.nsdc.org

Index

Note: An *f* following a page number indicates reference to a figure.

About the Authors

Jill Morgan is a research and training specialist in the Interdisciplinary Training Division at the Center for Persons with Disabilities, Utah State University, in Logan, Utah. **Betty Y. Ashbaker** is an assistant professor in Counseling Psychology and Special Education at Brigham Young University in Provo, Utah. Morgan and Ashbaker coauthored *The Effective Educator: A Training Program for Paraeducators; The Pro-Active Paraeducator: More Than 200 Really Nifty Ideas for People Who Help Teachers;* and *Teamwork and Self-Evaluation for Teachers and Paraeducators,* a training manual to help classroom teams develop their instructional skills and work together more effectively.

The authors have extensive experience in education. Jill Morgan has taught in elementary schools (general and special education) in urban and inner-city schools in the United Kingdom; Betty Ashbaker has experience as both a special education teacher and a district-level administrator. They now provide preservice and inservice training to teachers and paraeducators.

Jill Morgan may be reached at CPD-IDT, Utah State University, 6800 Old Main Hill, Logan, UT 84322-6800. E-mail: jmorgan@cc.usu.edu.

Betty Ashbaker may be reached at Counseling Psychology and Special Education, 332-H MCKB, P.O. Box 25093, Brigham Young University, Provo, UT 84602-5093. E-mail: Betty_Ashbaker@byu.edu.